THE VALUE OF COURAGE

The Value of Courage

Per Bauhn

NORDIC ACADEMIC PRESS

Nordic Academic Press
Box 1206
S-221 05 Lund, Sweden
Tel: +46 (0)46 33 34 50
Fax: +46 (0)46 18 96 85
E-mail: info@nordicacademicpress.com
www.nordicacademicpress.com

© Nordic Academic Press and the author 2003
Cover: Jacob Wiberg
Cover illustration: Painting by Franz von Stuck (1863–1928),
Judith and Holofernes (1926), Staatliches Museum, Schwerin.
Photo: Erich Lessing/IBL
Printed in Latvia
Preses Nams, Riga 2003
ISBN 91-89116-62-3

Table of Contents

Preface	7
1. The Need for Courage	9
2. Courage as the Ability to Confront Fear	29
3. The Courage of Creativity	45
4. The Courage of Conviction	61
The Fear of Meaninglessness	65
The Fear of Dying	70
The Fear of Social Death	84
5. The Objective Self and Moral Reasoning	91
6. The Common Good and Morality	107
7. Combining the Two Forms of Courage	119
Lewis	119
Robespierre	126
Irreconcilable Motivational Conflicts?	133
8. Heroism and Courage	137
The American Civil War Experience	149
Heroism and Ordinary Virtues	155
9. Prudence and Courage	167
10. Some Concluding Reflections on Courage	187
The Objection Regarding Courage as a Form of Sexism	187
The Objection Regarding Courage as a Cultivation of Insensitivity	192
The Objection Regarding Courage as Incapable of Dealing with Tragedy	195
Literature	205
Index	211

Preface

This is a philosophical study of courage. As such it contains an analysis of the concept of courage, a distinction between two forms of courage, and a discussion of the importance of courage to the good life and to moral life. The importance to individuals and to communities of the virtue of courage should by itself constitute a sufficient reason for writing a book like this one. However, a curious reader might suspect that behind the philosophical argument there is hidden a more personal story which, if revealed, would explain why the present writer chose to devote a whole book to the subject of confronting fears. In assuming this, the curious reader would be right. But since this is intended as a philosophical argument and not as a piece of autobiography, I will refrain from expanding on that theme. Moreover, bearing in mind that very common mistake in reasoning which is called the genetic fallacy, I believe that the *validity* of the claims put forward in this book can and should be assessed without invoking facts about their *origin* in the personal history of the writer.

In my work on this book I have incurred several debts of gratitude which I am happy to acknowledge. First of all, I would like to express my thanks to Alan Gewirth, who has for many years been my philosophical mentor, a constant source of inspiration and encouragement, and a perceptive partner in discussion. In letters as well as in conversation Alan has helped me to clarify my argument. He read the complete manuscript in its penultimate version and the exchange of ideas that we had in Chicago in March 2002 was a great help to me in preparing the final draft. Alan's comments have done a lot to make this a better book; if I had had more of his philosophical understanding and powers of reasoning it would have been better still.

I would also like to thank Christer Lindberg, long-time friend and colleague, who has read the complete manuscript and contributed to its improvement. I have also benefited from informal discussions with Carl-Göran Heidegren, Anja Hänsch, Svante Lundberg, and Thomas Malm. A summary of the argument of this book was presented to the Higher Seminar in Practical Philosophy, Lund University, in January 2002. Students of Peace and Conflict Studies have contributed their views on courage within the framework of a series of lectures entitled "Courage, Meaning, and Morality" that I gave at Lund University in 1999 and 2001.

My English has been checked and corrected by Alan Crozier and Duncan Smart. The final stage of my research was financed by the Swedish Royal Academy of Letters, History and Antiquities. Grants from the Erik and Gurli Hultengren Foundation for Philosophy and from the Crafoord Foundation contributed to the financing of the printing and publishing of the book.

Finally, I would like to express my gratitude to my parents, Gustaf and Karla Bauhn. My father, who died while I was working on this book, exemplified throughout his life a courageous individualism and a deep-seated love of personal freedom. Likewise, my mother has contributed to my understanding of courage by repeatedly proving to me that it is indeed possible to make something good come out of adverse circumstances. She is also a living example of the often ignored fact that courage is by no means incompatible with the "softer" virtues of compassion and empathy; on the contrary, courage may be fuelled by one's perception of other people being in need of one's support. For what I have learnt from them about courage, I am immensely grateful to my parents. This book is dedicated to them.

CHAPTER I

The Need for Courage

This is a book about the personal and moral importance of courage. As I will clarify in Chapter 2, courage should not be reduced to a martial virtue, emphasizing fearlessness in the face of physical danger, although it has implications for battlefield behaviour. I will argue that courage, generally speaking, is a disposition to confront fear (rather than being fearless), and that it is essential to the advancing of the personal good of the agent as well as of the common good of human communities. In this chapter I intend to present a background picture of why there is a need today for a discussion of the virtue of courage. In short, my argument will be that certain widely spread modern ailments, such as depression and feelings of alienation, can, at least in part, be understood as reactions to various depersonalizing conditions and beliefs present in contemporary social life that are likely to undermine people's sense of being autonomous agents. Courage is necessary to restore that sense.

Mankind's aspirations for a good life have faced various kinds of challenges at different times and in different societies. Once wars, plagues, famines, the abuse of tyrants, and the torments of hard physical labour constituted the major threats to human well-being. In many parts of the world this is still the case. However, even in modern democratic societies the good life may be endangered, not primarily by physical threats external to the human individual, such as war and starvation, but rather by psychological or motivational deficiencies, internal to the individual, such as depression, alienation, and lack of meaning. These internal deficiencies constitute a threat to the good life by undermining the individual's confidence in herself as an agent having goals worth achieving and as possessing the capacity to realize them.

Many people in modern societies seem to suffer from anxieties and distorted conceptions of themselves, manifested in a booming market for anti-depressants, and in the appearance of anorectic girls that seem to punish their bodies for not conforming to ideals of bodily perfection. In her best-selling book *Prozac Nation* Elizabeth Wurtzel relates a report that pictures depression as a particular affliction of our times:

> Those born after 1955 are *three times* as likely as their grandparents' generation to suffer from depression. In fact, of Americans born before 1905, only one percent had experienced a depression episode by age seventy-five, while of those born after 1955, six percent were already depressed by age twenty-four. Apparently, the trend is global, with studies in Italy, Germany, Taiwan, Lebanon, Canada, France, New Zealand, Puerto Rico, and elsewhere yielding similar numbers. (Wurtzel, p. 337. The figures given by Wurtzel are also in Goleman, p. 276; Goleman also provides the source: Lewinsohn, Peter, et al., "Age-Cohort Changes in the Lifetime Occurrence of Depression and Other Mental Disorders", *Journal of Abnormal Psychology* 102 (1993).)

A similar picture is given by consultant psychiatrist Paul Crichton:

> There has been an overall increase in serious depression in Americans born since the Second World War. A similar increase has been found in Munich, Florence, Paris, Beirut, Taiwan and New Zealand. The psychiatrist David Healy has estimated that in 1896, 20 per cent of the psychiatric patients admitted in north Wales had been given a diagnosis of melancholia and that most of them, about forty per million, would now be diagnosed as suffering from a major depressive disorder with psychotic symptoms. The equivalent figure today would be 948 per million, a twenty-four-fold increase. At a press conference on the publication of his recent annual report, *The State of Public Health 1997*, the former Chief Medical Officer, Sir Kenneth Calman, is reported to have stated that between 1994 and 1996 there had been a 15 per cent increase in the number of women in England and Wales on antidepressants and a 19 per cent

increase in the number of men. He wondered whether the demands of modern life could be a cause. (Crichton, p. 14.)

Moreover, psychological studies indicate that, in children, depression seems to be caused by a pessimistic conviction that there is nothing they can do to improve their lot:

> The most direct evidence that a pessimistic outlook makes children highly susceptible to depression comes from a five-year study of children beginning when they were in third grade.... As the children grew through the elementary-school years, there was a telling shift in their thinking about the good and bad events of their lives, with the children increasingly ascribing them to their own traits: "I'm getting good grades because I'm smart"; "I don't have many friends because I'm no fun." This shift seems to set in gradually over the third to fifth grades. As this happens those children who develop a pessimistic outlook – attributing the setbacks in their lives to some dire flaw in themselves – begin to fall prey to depressed moods in reaction to setbacks. What's more, the experience of depression itself seems to reinforce these pessimistic ways of thinking, so that even after the depression lifts, the child is left with what amounts to an emotional scar, a set of convictions fed by the depression and solidified in the mind: that he can't do well in school, is unlikable, and can do nothing to escape his own brooding moods. These fixed ideas can make the child all the more vulnerable to another depression down the road. (Goleman, p. 281.)

These findings suggest that we should pay attention to those factors of social life that may affect people's conception of themselves, in order to understand important aspects of their mental well-being. We should not reject the possibility that there might be aspects of the modern condition that may well have an adverse impact on people's sense of autonomy and meaning. One idea that has been put forward is that modern men and women are too self-centred in their interactions with the external world, thereby disconnecting themselves from conceptions of the common good and other moral ideals from which earlier generations were able to derive meaning in their lives. A possible explanation of the contemporary incidence of depressive illnesses would then be to point to the effects of an excessive individualism. Charles Taylor seems to adhere to this theory:

> The worry has been repeatedly expressed that the individual lost something important along with the larger social and cosmic horizons of action. Some have written of this as the loss of a heroic dimension to life. People no longer have a sense of a higher purpose, of something worth dying for....
>
> This loss of purpose was linked to a narrowing. People lost the broader vision because they focussed on their individual lives.... In other words, the dark side of individualism is a centring on the self, which both flattens and narrows our lives, makes them poorer in meaning, and less concerned with others or society. (Taylor, 1991, pp. 3–4.)

Moreover, the pervasiveness and rapidity of socio-technological change characteristic of contemporary society may cause at least some people to question their ability to control their destiny, and so bring about their despair. Not only will they find that the way of doing things they were used to is rendered obsolete by new technology, but the very pace of change will make it hard for them to catch up. These people may face the choice of either being subjected to recurrent retraining programmes, haunted by the slogans of the new era about the importance of "flexibility" and "lifelong learning", or being left permanently behind, stuck with low-paid jobs or no jobs at all.

> With ever-changing technology, people need ever-changing skills – yet even in the richest countries many lack the basics. Despite universal primary and secondary education in OECD countries, one person in six is functionally illiterate – unable to fill out a job application, excluded from the rapidly changing world that demands new skills in processing information. With unemployment a luxury few can afford, people who cannot get formal employment end up in the informal sector....

> As multinationals merge, corporate restructuring means job losses.... Though the loss of corporate jobs may be compensated by employment creation elsewhere, it adds to the insecurity of people in their jobs and lives. (*Human Development Report 1999*, p. 37.)

And the mental stress emanating from workplaces where the employees both are under pressure to perform efficiently and lack control over the conditions of their work is likely to render people vulnerable to serious health problems:

> For example, Stephen Manuck, a University of Pittsburgh psychologist, put thirty volunteers through a vigorous, anxiety-riddled ordeal in a laboratory while he monitored the men's blood, assaying a substance secreted by blood platelets called adenosine triphosphate, or ATP, which can trigger blood-vessel changes that may lead to heart attacks and strokes. While the volunteers were under the intense stress, their ATP levels rose sharply, as did their heart rate and blood pressure.
>
> Understandably, health risks seem greatest for those whose jobs are high in "strain": having high-pressure performance demands while having little or no control over how to get the job done (a predicament that gives bus drivers, for instance, a high rate of hypertension). For example, in a study of 569 patients with colorectal cancer and a matched comparison group, those who said that in the previous ten years they had experienced severe on-the-job aggravation were five and a half times more likely to have developed the cancer compared to those with no such stress in their lives. (Goleman, p. 200.)

To some extent, we are already subjected to the decisions of machines, the impact of which may sometimes be disastrous:

> In the Black Monday UK stock market crash of October 1987, machines had been programmed to sell shares when they fell below a preset price. Certain shares did so fall and the resultant selling triggered further mass selling, which caused an even faster drop in prices. In humans, this would be called a panic reaction, but

machines don't panic, do they? Given that they all have roughly similar goals, more and more such machine panic runs are likely. (Warwick, p. 125.)

The idea that technological developments may be harmful to the self-image of people whose condition is such that they are subjected to them rather than in control of them, is a classic piece of the criticism of the process of civilization. Max Weber, for instance, saw a loss of humanity immanent in the specialization required by capitalist production, where man's condition is determined by the machines he has to serve:

> Limitation to specialized work, with a renunciation of the Faustian universality of man which it involves, is a condition of any valuable work in the modern world; hence deeds and renunciation inevitably condition each other to-day....
>
> The Puritan wanted to work in a calling; we are forced to do so. For when asceticism was carried out of monastic cells into everyday life, and began to dominate worldly morality, it did its part in building the tremendous cosmos of the modern economic order. This order is now bound to the technical and economic conditions of machine production which to-day determine the lives of all the individuals who are born into this mechanism, not only those directly concerned with economic acquisition, with irresistible force. Perhaps it will so determine them until the last ton of fossilized coal is burnt. In Baxter's view the care for external goods should only lie on the shoulders of the "saint like a light cloak, which can be thrown aside at any moment". But fate decreed that the cloak should become an iron cage. (Weber, pp. 180–181; Richard Baxter, 1615–91, was an English Puritan theologian.)

The threat of modern capitalism to human well-being and autonomy is also, of course, a central aspect of Marx's discussion of the alienation of the worker:

> The worker becomes all the poorer the more wealth he produces, the more his production increases in power and size. The worker

> becomes an ever cheaper commodity the more commodities he creates. The *devaluation* of the world of men is in direct proportion to the *increasing value* of the world of things. Labour produces not only commodities: it produces itself and the worker as a *commodity* – and this at the same rate at which it produces commodities in general.... Therefore the greater this product, the less is he himself. The *alienation* of the worker in his product means not only that his labour becomes an object, an *external* existence, but that it exists *outside him*, independently, as something alien to him, and that it becomes a power on its own confronting him. It means that the life which he has conferred on the object confronts him as something hostile and alien. (Marx, pp. 271–272.)

Where alienation once meant being a stranger to the products of one's work, it may now imply being or becoming a stranger to one's social environment as this environment becomes ever more infused with a computerized technology the workings and consequences of which may be hard to comprehend. People may come to perceive the world they live in as no longer theirs, but rather as a world in which a lot of their options are determined by machines which they can neither do without, nor fully understand, generating effects which they feel they can neither fully control, nor escape. Moreover, the fear of technological failure will take on a more sinister appearance, if it turns out that people are not only utterly dependent on computer technology but utterly helpless if something goes wrong with it. It need not be anything as dramatic as a third world war initiated by computer error. It is bad enough to know that the heating of one's home may suddenly fail to work in the winter, or that one's bank savings may be wiped out, due to an erratic program in some distant central computer. Given that people are indeed this vulnerable, and given that they become aware of their vulnerability, it might turn out that the computer era will contribute to undermine people's sense of personal autonomy in a way similar to the process depicted by Marx long ago.

Add to this the vast organizational structures of the modern world, with their bureaucracies and intricate regulations, which may well make the individual person feel even more insignificant and helpless. The requirements of a bureaucratized and specialized society tend not only to limit individual freedom, but also to depersonalize society by their insistence on uniform and standardized procedures. This depersonalization is also manifested in a certain form of modern city architecture, with mass-produced suburban housing constructions, in the form of tall geometrical boxes, all of them sharing the same exterior features, making them virtually impossible to individuate. Commenting on two modern Stockholm suburbs, Doreen Yarwood observes that

> Swedish post-war architecture has produced some remarkably banal results from such high powered planning and automation. The advanced methods of construction seem to have created only dull, circumscribed buildings, markedly so in contrast to the lively, original and beautifully finished work of the Finns. *Vällingby New Town*, for instance, today gives an impression of a small, unnotable town centre, with functional and well-constructed buildings, but drab in both style and hue. The whole town displays a marked lack of imagination, in appearance and in design. Everything is in grey and dun. Concrete and dull brown brick prevail. The churches are as unecclesiastical as garages and as unwelcoming. They look as though they were produced as cheaply and quickly as possible. *Farsta New Town* is similar but poorer, both architecturally and in quality of building and workmanship. Though later, already it is shabbier than Vällingby. In both towns the main housing near the centre is in stark, high-rise concrete blocks built, like so many others in different countries, before the planners of Europe 'discovered' that most people prefer, and need, to live in low rise blocks, or even small houses. (Yarwood, p. 544.)

This is the architecture of an unsentimental functionalism, aspiring to a maximally efficient use of expensive urban space. It is no coincidence that the architects of functionalism abhorred ornamentation and decorations on buildings. Being unnecessary to the ideal of efficient and scientific management of society, they were discarded as remnants of an individualist bourgeois sentimentality, belonging to an irrational and romantic aesthetics, which was to be replaced by the ideal of streamlining, endorsed not only by social engineers, but also by the intellectual avant-garde of the early twentieth century.

It should be noted in this context that some aesthetically radical Russian intellectuals (including the painter Kazimir Malevich) welcomed the Revolution of 1917, because "they felt that their geometric, analytical forms were linked directly to the world of technological efficiency and mechanical wizardry that they identified with the immediate future" (Bowlt, p. 57). One of these avant-garde intellectuals, Boris Arvatov, had a vision of a proletarian city, characterized by "total streamlining", providing its inhabitants with moving pavements, automatic restaurants, and clothes with detachable parts:

> Clearly, the consumer of these superobjects would also have to be mechanized and efficient, and just such a development was undertaken and planned at the Central Institute of Labor (TsIT) in Moscow, supervised by Alexei Gastev, aided by the poet Ippolit Sokolov, and supported by Malevich. One of many curious institutions of the postrevolutionary years, TsIT aspired to produce a program of rhythmical, economical movements for the factory floor such as hammering, welding, and working a lathe. TsIT maintained, as the constructivists did, that function determined form and that the Communist way of doing things should be the rational, streamlined way that would avoid the capricious gesture with its unnecessary expenditure of energy. (Bowlt, p. 57.)

In their architecture, European functionalists continued this cult of efficiency and standardization. When these ideals were applied to city planning, they sometimes resulted in buildings that appear as towers of homogenization rather than as homes expressing the individuality of the persons living there.

Now, the pervasiveness of modern network technology, the ever increasing speed of technological change, the vast centralized bureaucratic structures needed to administrate a complex modern society, and an anti-individualist social framework emphasizing "streamlining", may constitute a formidable challenge to people's confidence in their ability to control their social environment, and hence to their autonomy. The individual human being is supposed to adjust to the fact that she is subjected to constant *liminality*, that is, the condition of constantly moving from one stage of socio-technological development to another. And, obviously, the condition of liminality may be detrimental to the good life of the individual human being, as it may undermine her confidence in herself as an agent, controlling her own destiny in accordance with her own choices and actions. Liminality hence may add to alienation in circumscribing personal autonomy. (The concept of liminality was originally applied by Victor Turner to what takes place in rites of passage, during which the state of the ritual subject is ambiguous as she "passes through a realm that has few or none of the attributes of the past or coming state" (Turner, p. 94). I am very grateful to Anja Hänsch for making me see the relevance of the concept of liminality to the present work.)

Now, in addition to the possible negative impacts of socio-technological developments on the self-image of modern men and women, there are influential contemporary conceptions of human nature and the human condition that seem to give little room for a belief in individual autonomy and self-assertion. For one thing, a widespread preoccupation with avoiding risks and a general sense of being exposed to various kinds of threats, whether in the form of a polluted environment, genetically modified food, contagious and fatal diseases, negligent doctors, or malevolent strangers, tend to engulf us in what sociologist Frank Furedi has called a "culture of fear":

> Today, the fear of taking risks is creating a society that celebrates victimhood rather than heroism. We are all expected to compete, like guests on a television programme, to prove that we are the most put-upon and pathetic people in the house, the most deserving of counselling and compensation. The virtues held up to be followed are passivity rather than activism, safety rather than boldness. And the rather diminished individual that emerges is indulged on the grounds that, in a world awash with conditions and crises and impending catastrophe, he or she is doing a good job just by surviving. (Furedi, p. 13.)

Moreover, according to a certain biologistic approach to man, which emphasizes the importance of our genetic makeup in the explanation of human behaviour, the idea that we can control our lives is more or less an illusion. In fact, this form of biologism asserts, we are controlled by our genes. Nature, not the way we live, makes us depressed or criminal. Hereditary traits, not intentions and desires, decide what we will do. In the words of James D. Watson, famous co-discoverer of the structure of the DNA molecule, "our fate is in our genes" (quoted in Kaye, p. 45).

Likewise, Edward O. Wilson has argued that "the mind is the brain at work and, as such, can be understood entirely as a biological phenomenon" (Wilson, p. 137). This means, according to Wilson, that "[w]hat we think of as meaning is the linkage among neural networks" (p. 140), and since culture is learned and "learning is genetically biased" (p. 141), it follows that "biology is the logical foundational discipline of the social sciences" (p. 145).

Now, it is one thing to claim that human nature as well as human culture(s) have a history, and that although our emotional life is coloured by the cultural context in which it has developed, there would be nothing for culture to colour if it were not for the fact that we are biologically endowed with a capacity for an emotional life. But it is a different thing altogether to claim that cultural understanding can be *reduced* to biological understanding. We may accept that our history as biological beings is much older than our history as cultural beings, and that "corporate CEOs impelled by stone-age emotions work international deals with cellular telephones at thirty thousand feet" (Wilson, pp. 144–145). But the fact that the *capacity* for emotions like love and anger is biologically given is not, by itself, more important for our understanding of ourselves as human beings than the fact that the ways in which these emotions are *expressed* are influenced by various cultural contexts and by individual choices within these contexts.

More importantly, if we reduce culture to nature, and sociology to biology, we will also reduce agency to "neural networks". That is, our conception of man will no longer be that of an agent whose behaviour is guided by her intentions and purposes, but rather that of a recipient of genetic conditioning. But this development would represent a narrowing of perspective, not an increase in understanding. Wilson argues that "it is hard to imagine how the social sciences can unite and achieve general, predictive theory without taking a reductionist approach to the phenomena of human nature" (p. 146). But this line of arguing presupposes of course that the goal of the social sciences *is* to "achieve general, predictive theory". But what if the purpose of these sciences, as well as of the humanities, is instead to enrich our understanding of the complexities of human life, as these are manifested in individual and social action, guided by various moral, aesthetic, political, religious, and other kinds of norms? Then Wilson's reductionism would appear simply as a fallacy, identifying a complex outcome with one of its necessary preconditions.

Now, while it is of course important that we learn as much as we can about ourselves from biology, it is just as important that we do not get seduced by a biologistic metaphysics, which goes beyond the scientific data to pronounce on how we should conceive of ourselves and our possibilities to affect outcomes by our own agency. It is, for instance, one thing to assert that depression correlates with deficiencies in the serotonin level in the brain. It is quite another to say that depression is *nothing but* a deficiency in the serotonin level, and that the sole cure for depression is medication aimed at restoring the right level of serotonin. It is one thing to identify a certain gene correlated with "pleasure-seeking activity" that may indirectly contribute to the alcoholism of some individuals; it is quite another to say that alcoholism is genetically caused, and that no interventions other than medical ones can cure alcoholics. To go from the reasonable idea that biology may *influence* our behaviour in various ways to the unfounded conclusion that biology *determines* our behaviour, is not only an erroneous piece of metaphysics. It is also a morally problematic view as it may well undermine people's confidence in their own powers of doing something with their lives, and hence deprive them of the fulfilment achieved by successfully confronting obstacles.

And, as psychologist Daniel Goleman points out, even if we accept that there are innate emotional patterns, this does not mean that we have to accept that there is nothing we can do to control our ways of reacting to the world:

> A child who comes into the world easily frightened can learn to be calmer, or even outgoing, in the face of the unfamiliar. Fearfulness – or any other temperament – may be part of the biological givens of our emotional lives, but we are not necessarily limited to a specific emotional menu by our inherited traits. There is a range of possibility even within genetic constraints. (Goleman, p. 256.)

Moreover, the idea, derived from the biologistic reductionism described above, that social and psychological problems should be subjected to medical treatment or genetic engineering may well come to endanger the dignity of individuals. The same drive for efficiency that in other areas of modern life has subordinated individuals to machines and to centralized bureaucratic structures, may now subordinate them to the interference of neuroscientists and psychiatrists. Referring to a study that allegedly gives support to the idea that alcoholism might be genetically caused and hence a proper target for genetic engineering, Howard Kaye comments:

> Leaving aside the smallness of the sample-size; forgetting for a moment that the gene identified seems to be correlated with "pleasure-seeking activity" in general and not simply some cases of alcoholism; ignoring temporarily the potentially devastating, stigmatizing effects of such screening and the possible effects of any drug therapy, there is still the shocking lack of awareness that the question of the "best way" to treat a problem such as alcoholism is not purely a question of efficiency, speed, or cost. It is a moral and political question as well, provided, of course, that we recognize that we are dealing both with a problem which has important social, cultural, and psychological causes and with a being who possesses a potentially free and responsible soul that ought to be respected. It may even be possible that the "best way" morally to treat such a person may not be the most cost-effective way. (Kaye, pp. 46–47.)

However, the relationship between modernity and the good life should not be understood only in the negative terms of modernity undermining individual self-confidence and autonomy. There is also another and more positive aspect of modernity, emphasizing individuality, agency, reason, progress, and freedom. Hence, we have not only the image of the helpless and vulnerable individual described above, whose life is controlled by an impersonal and more or less deterministic socio-technological development. We have also the image of the self-assertive individual who, having freed herself from the shackles of superstition and tradition, is eager to explore the possibilities of the world and to be an *agent* rather than a *recipient* of her destiny.

This individualist spirit is manifested in the admiration bestowed on explorers of the Victorian era (for instance, Livingstone, Stanley, Shackleton, Nansen, Amundsen), as well as in the cult of the artistic genius (Wagner) and in the conception of the overman (Nietzsche), but modern individualism is not only an élite phenomenon. As people have moved from rural areas to urban ones, and as legal, political, technological, medical, and economic conditions have changed in a way that allows the individual more options, there has been a general increase in freedom of choice as well as an increased awareness of the value and importance of this freedom. This would be seen, I believe, from a simple comparison between the lives of, let us say, an average middle-class woman or an average working-class man living one hundred years ago, and the lives of their counterparts today.

The more extreme form of the individualism associated with the Victorian era, and manifested in the character of the hero, was more or less discredited by the two world wars. World War I quickly evolved into a great slaughter which made it clear that the individual counted for very little in modern warfare. In the Battle of the Somme in 1916, the British lost more than 400,000 men, while the Germans lost 281,000 at Verdun in the same year. All in all, thirteen million lives were lost during four years of war. And as the reality of the battlefield pierced through the myths of national propaganda, "[t]he enthusiasm of 1914 became the disillusionment of 1916" (Mosse, p. 68).

Hence, the initial optimism of the soldiers going to war in 1914, many of them volunteers, came to appear as an appalling delusion, caused by a cult of heroism. The words of British poet Rupert Brooke (who died of blood-poisoning in 1915, during the Gallipoli expedition, at the age of twenty-eight) to a friend at the beginning of the war: "Come and die. It'll be great fun" (quoted in Walzer, p. 26 n.) contain all the recklessness later associated with heroism.

The experiences of World War I contributed to a general rejection of all heroic rhetoric, as when the poet Herbert Read in 1928 condemned the prose of Winston Churchill's *World Crisis* as falsely eloquent and derived from an "aggrandisation of the self" instead of an "aggrandisation of the theme". And, as Isaiah Berlin notes in his essay on Churchill,

> This view was well received by the young men who were painfully reacting against anything which appeared to go beyond the naked skeleton of the truth, at a time when not only rhetoric but even noble eloquence seemed outrageous hypocrisy. Churchill's critic spoke, and knew that he spoke, for a post-war generation; the psychological symptoms of the vast and rapid social transformation then in progress, from which the government in power so resolutely averted its gaze, were visible to the least discerning critics of literature and the arts; the mood was dissatisfied, hostile and insecure; the sequel to so much magnificence was too bitter, and left behind it a heritage of hatred for the grand style as such. The victims and casualties of the disaster thought they had earned the right to be rid of the trappings of an age which had heartlessly betrayed them. (Berlin, p. 2.)

World War II revealed how the cult of heroic self-sacrifice could become a tool for a ruthless Nazi dictatorship, as epitomized not only by fanatical SS soldiers but also by those teenagers who defended Berlin in the last days of the Third Reich. As Philip M. Taylor points out in his history of propaganda, these *Hitlerjunge* were indeed "Hitler's children", living proofs of totalitarianism and a thoroughly militarized society (Taylor, 1995, p. 241). After the end of the war, Germans themselves in the western zones of occupation suggested that new war memorials should no longer refer to national martyrs, but simply to "our dead" (Mosse, p. 212).

The experiences of the great wars of the twentieth century may suffice to explain why modernity turned its back on individual heroism, and instead set its hopes on technological development which, in combination with an enlightened social engineering, would bring welfare to all. Restrictions regarding individual autonomy could in this context not only be justified, but indeed welcomed, as unbridled individualism in the form of heroism, was held at least partially responsible for the disasters of World War I. The belief that technology and social engineering were needed to control human irrationality was reinforced by the events of World War II and the presence of nuclear weapons after 1945. Hence, B. F. Skinner could, as late as 1971, defend the need for a "technology of behaviour", with explicit anti-individualist implications:

> The traditional conception of man [as an autonomous agent] is flattering; it confers reinforcing privileges. It is therefore easily defended and can be changed only with difficulty. It was designed to build up the individual as an instrument of counter-control, and it did so effectively but in such a way as to limit progress. We have seen how the literatures of freedom and dignity, with their concern for autonomous man, have perpetuated the use of punishment and condoned the use of only weak nonpunitive techniques, and it is not difficult to demonstrate a connection between the unlimited right of the individual to pursue happiness and the catastrophes threatened by unchecked breeding, the unrestrained affluence which exhausts resources and pollutes the environment, and the imminence of nuclear war. (Skinner, p. 213.)

Skinner believed that talk of autonomy, intentions, purposes, and agency represented a "prescientific way" of thinking (p. 9), and that the existence of autonomous man "depends upon our ignorance, and he naturally loses status as we come to know more about behavior" (p. 14). As our understanding of human behaviour improves, Skinner argues, we will come to see that it is produced by conditions external to the individual. The individual is presented by Skinner as reacting rather than acting, and her emotions and intentions are explicitly rejected as explanatory factors:

> The punishment of sexual behavior changes sexual *behavior*, and any feelings which may arise are at best by-products. Our age is not suffering from anxiety but from the accidents, crimes, wars, and other dangerous and painful things to which people are so often exposed. Young people drop out of school, refuse to get jobs, and associate only with others of their own age not because they feel alienated but because of defective social environments in homes, schools, factories, and elsewhere. (Skinner, pp. 14–15.)

But clearly something is amiss with Skinner's argument here. He consistently employs words indicating *actions* – young people *drop* out of school, they *refuse* to get jobs, they *associate* with others – and yet he concludes that their ways of conceiving of their situation are inconsequential. Skinner seems to endorse a mechanical causality, unaffected by emotions and intentions, but what he actually describes is *agency*, that is, not only behaviour but *purposive* behaviour, reflecting the intentions, emotions, and values of persons who want to achieve certain ends. And the presence of external conditions, such as "defective social environments", is *not* inconsistent with the presence of conditions internal to the agent, such as feelings of alienation. On the contrary, without any such internal conditions it would be difficult to understand why a certain set of external conditions would result in any of the above behaviours in the first place.

To sum up the discussion so far, while many modern people seem to suffer from depressive illnesses and while there is reason to believe that certain alienating features of contemporary social life may contribute to their ailment by depriving their lives of a sense of autonomy and meaning, they are also presented with a view of the world according to which they either could not or should not assert themselves as individual agents. While biologism seems to reject the idea of individual autonomy as being inconsistent with genetic determinism, a certain behaviourist ethics of social engineering not only rejects autonomy as inconsistent with a "scientific" understanding of human behaviour, but also condemns the idea of autonomy as a normative ideal, as it is believed to result in selfishness and chauvinism. This ethical objection to the idea of individual autonomy feeds on the heroic exaggerations manifested in and causally related to the great wars of the twentieth century.

However, as we noted above, there are reasons for not accepting the biologistic rejection of individual autonomy, as this rejection is based on a too simplistic view of human nature. Likewise, the mechanical view of human agency advanced by behaviourism seems to be internally inconsistent as well as lacking in explanatory power. And as regards the ethical objection to individualism and heroism, we could argue that its target should not be individual autonomy *per se*, but rather certain *interpretations* of individual autonomy, such as in Nietzsche's identification of freedom with the agent's "drive for power" (Nietzsche, pp. 383–384). Hence, we may well accept the ethical objection to élitist and selfish interpretations of autonomy, without having to reject *all* versions of individual autonomy.

Autonomy is, among other things, about preserving our status as agents and about our being able to conceive of ourselves as agents. Accordingly, autonomy entails not only the ability to be in control of oneself, having one's actions guided by purposes of one's own unforced choice, but also a *sense* of autonomy and of self-respect and dignity appropriate to one who is able to exercise this basic form of self-control. Hence, autonomy is essential to the good life of any human being, as it is a necessary component of objective as well as subjective dimensions of agency.

Now, a person's sense of autonomy may be endangered not only by adverse social or natural conditions, but also by her lack of confidence in her powers of agency. Especially prominent here are various kinds of fear, which may either completely paralyse the agent in certain contexts, or at least severely diminish her capacity for agency. While a fear of failure or a generalized fear of becoming a victim (of accidents, illnesses, the harmful actions of other people, etc.) may have its roots in causes and conditions external to the agent, once the agent gives in to her fears she is likely to find herself even more incapable and subjected to limitations as regards her agency, which in turn will increase her fears, leading to a further decrease in confidence, and so on.

Hence, the ability to resist fear is indeed of the utmost importance to all agents. And while the desire to resist fear may occasionally turn into an exaggerated cult of heroism, this is by no means a necessary outcome. Hence, to the extent that we accept that individual autonomy is indeed an essential component of the good life of any human agent, we should also accept that the good life requires *courage*, since courage enables the agent to resist fear and to that extent also enables her to remain and conceive of herself as an agent.

However, courage too has been viewed with a certain scepticism by some modern philosophers. In 1963 Richard Hare, for instance, argued that "[i]t would be a hazardous claim, at any rate in modern society, that the moral quality of so-called 'physical' courage is on the whole conducive to human well-being" (Hare, p. 149).

Now, Hare obviously thought of courage as a battlefield quality, as can be seen from his statement that although courage may once have been vital to the preservation of society, this may no longer be the case "in the present state of military science" (ibid.). However, Hare ignores the fact that courage has applications outside the martial context, and that it is indeed necessary to the realization of any reasonably fulfilling life. As Peter Geach notes:

> For a start, as Chesterton remarked, people would often not be born but for the courage of their mothers; this truth is more obvious nowadays when motherhood is more a matter of choice.... Even apart from the risk that childbearing will result in death or in permanent physical impairment, carrying a baby to full term may call for considerable endurance.... Again, our bodies are highly vulnerable, constantly exposed to peril of injury and death; but if we were always worrying about how to protect them, we should be cut off from very many activities, lose much enjoyment, suffer many inconveniences, and be continually plagued by painful apprehension. Nobody who was thoroughly cowardly would play physically demanding games, or climb a mountain, or ride a horse or a bicycle.... [A] modicum of courage is needed by the least athletic of us if he is to live in a modern city. (Geach, pp. 151–152.)

Courage, when contrasted with its extreme form, rashness, as well as with its opposite, cowardice, is indeed a kind of strength, as John Mackie has observed:

> It makes its possessor more likely to achieve whatever he sets out to do, whereas the foolhardy man is likely to destroy himself or his enterprise or both, and the timid man is too easily turned aside. Besides, most worthwhile enterprises involve risks of some kind, and the courageous man can enjoy the activity, risks and all, whereas the coward cannot.... To be a coward on the one occasion when courage is fatal one would have had to be a coward on many other occasions when it was much better to be courageous. (Mackie, p. 189.)

Accordingly, the fact that an individual may use her autonomy for morally bad purposes, and the fact that an inflated belief in individual autonomy may result in an exaggerated conception of personal responsibility that can be invoked to justify excessive and unwarranted punitive measures, do not rule out that autonomy is also a central aspect of the good life of man. And although there is no reason why we should adopt the martial heroism of the Victorian era, there is something to be said for a view of man and society that not only respects but actually encourages self-confidence and dedication to goals beyond the satisfaction of strictly personal preferences. In short, and in line with the reasoning above, I believe that the good life presupposes the virtue of courage.

CHAPTER 2

Courage as the Ability to Confront Fear

In this chapter I will propose a definition of the term "courage", and also discuss how the concept of courage is related to the concepts of fear and danger. Moreover, I will make some preliminary remarks regarding the relationship between courage and morality.

By "courage" I mean the ability of an agent to confront fear in the pursuit of her goals. As for the defining term "fear", I intend to distinguish between two kinds of fear, corresponding to two kinds of courage to be discussed below. The first kind of fear is the *fear of failure*, which will, when sufficiently strong, prevent the agent from pursuing her goal by making her very sensitive to the possibility that she may fail, as well as making her expect such failure to have disastrous consequences. The second kind of fear is the *fear of personal transience*, which involves not only a fear of dying and of suffering bodily injury, but also a fear of social ostracism, as well as a fear that one's life is insignificant, meaningless, making no difference whatsoever in the world. The fear of personal transience may severely handicap an agent by making her unwilling to take risks, irrespective of the importance of the goal. Believing that it will not matter whether she acts or does not act, and scared by the possibility that she may herself be victimized, the agent may refuse to stand up for a friend who is being persecuted, or refrain from taking a stand against oppressive activities going on in her society. Moreover, the fear of personal transience tends to be self-reinforcing, as it isolates the agent from important collective undertakings that involve physical risks (such as fighting for freedom and justice in an oppressive society), and thereby also deprives her of the sense of significance pertaining to those who can see themselves as contributing to some important common good. Hence, the agent's fear of victimization breeds a passivity, which in turn generates a lowered self-esteem that reinforces her passivity, but now supported by her belief that she cannot make a difference.

It should be noted that, while courage is here defined in terms of being able to confront *fear*, this is not equivalent to saying that courage is about confronting *danger*. Although danger (in the sense of a serious threat to one's life, health, or basic conditions of life) may be a common cause of fear, this is by no means always the case. Some agents fear things that are not really dangerous (such as losing some person's love), while some other agents do not fear things that are really dangerous (such as taking drugs). Of course, we could argue that "danger" should be given a purely subjective interpretation, implying that if P believes that x is dangerous, then x constitutes a danger to P. However, since I believe that it is important to be able to criticize a person's beliefs regarding what is or is not dangerous ("You are wrong – this insect is not dangerous!"), I will not opt for a subjective interpretation of the concept of danger. Moreover, I will leave room for the concept of courage to apply regardless of whether there really is something dangerous or not to confront. Hence, when assessing a person's courage, I will allow room for the agent's subjective beliefs in a way that I am not prepared to do when it comes to assessing danger. We should not deny that an agent is courageous when she confronts *her* fear of *x*, although we believe that her beliefs regarding the fearsome features of *x* are wrong. Hence, while courage is about confronting fear, it is not necessarily about confronting danger. Here I disagree with Douglas Walton, who argues that

> a courageous action need not be defined in terms of the psychological property of fear. A courageous act is one in which, based on the good intentions of the agent in attempting to realize a worthy goal, he or she overcomes great danger or difficulty – whether afraid or not. (Walton, p. 14.)

Now, it could be argued that there is an intermediate position between defining courage in terms of the ability to confront (subjective) fear, and defining courage in terms of the ability to confront (objective) danger. James D. Wallace seems to defend such an intermediate position, as he defines courage in terms of the agent's *belief* that what she is about to do is dangerous to her. Hence, courage depends in part on the agent's perception of the situation at hand, and is to that extent subjectively defined: "Someone who sees no peril in what he does is not acting courageously" (Wallace, p. 78). However, Wallace adds the requirement that other people must confirm the agent's judgement that the situation at hand is dangerous in order for the agent's behaviour to be courageous: "The danger A sees in doing Y must be sufficiently formidable that most people would find it difficult in the circumstances to do Y" (Wallace, p. 79). But then Wallace goes on to make a move that seems to confuse his reasoning so far:

> An agent, in performing a courageous act, need not feel any fear at all, nor need he feel the act difficult. We admire the courage of someone who does something very dangerous so coolly that it appears to be easy for him. It is necessary, however, in order for his act to be courageous, that he be aware of the danger and that he recognize it as a danger. (Wallace, p. 80.)

Wallace seems to hold that although the courageous agent must "see" some peril in what she is about to do, and although this peril should be "formidable" enough for other people to find the agent's undertaking difficult, still the agent need not feel any fear at all. Hence, the subjective dimension of Wallace's definition has no necessary emotional content at all, but could be reduced to a mere calculus or estimate regarding the dangers involved.

But what is admired in a courageous act is not, I believe, just the carrying out of a dangerous action. We would not call a robot courageous for walking across a minefield. And the reason why we do not is that the robot, being the machine it is, has no emotional capacity, and hence cannot feel either fear or pain. Hence, in the case of the robot there can be no confrontation of fears. But it is precisely her ability to confront her fears that we admire in the courageous agent, not just her ability to go through with a dangerous mission. A person who is insensitive to fear (in this respect resembling the robot) and for this reason is capable of walking across a minefield without the slightest hesitation, will make us question her sanity rather than causing us to admire her courage. Psychological numbness in the face of great danger is an indication of mental disorder, rather than a virtue. Where there is no fear, there can be no courage, since courage is, I believe, about mastering (which is not necessarily the same as extinguishing) one's fears.

Moreover, the courageous option may not always be the most dangerous one, but rather the one that involves the most patience and hard work. To work oneself out of a slum condition or to defy one's craving for drugs, in both cases after having confronted a strong fear that one will fail (perhaps because one has failed before, or because one's family and friends expect one to fail) would indeed be instances of courage. Yet it could be plausibly argued that there is more danger involved in remaining in the slum, or in giving in to one's craving for drugs, than in trying to break free from these living conditions. Still, it is unlikely that we should conclude in these cases that courage is where the danger is, and that it would be more courageous to remain in the slum and go on using drugs than to quit the slum and give up the drugs.

Now, it may be objected that it is the value of the goal that determines whether the efforts to achieve it deserve the name of courage. That is why we call the efforts to break free from the slum or to quit using drugs courageous, while we refrain from calling the opposite behaviour this, although the latter may well be more dangerous. We simply find it praiseworthy to work oneself out of the slum and to abstain from drugs, and this is the reason why we call these endeavours courageous.

However, while this may well be true of how people often reason in matters like these, it does not reflect the conception of courage defended here. According to this conception, courage is about the efforts expended by an agent to pursue her goals in the face of her fears of failure and personal transience, not about the value of the goals themselves. Moreover, it seems strange that we should have to know about the goodness of the agent's goals in order to take a position on her courage. This is especially problematic since people may find it harder to agree on what makes a goal valuable than on the psychological qualities of the agent trying to achieve it.

Sometimes we may simply not know enough about the agent's goal or about the long-term consequences of her action to be able to pronounce on its overall value. Suppose that someone in the late 1890s saved a child from a burning house, confronting her fear of personal transience in the operation, and that this child was Adolf Hitler. Would our knowledge of Hitler's later career force us to deny that the person saving little Adolf's life was courageous? Clearly, this would be absurd. Nothing that Hitler the dictator would later do could undo the courage of the person who saved little Adolf.

Well, it may be objected, this may be true given a distinction between the moral value of trying to achieve a particular goal and the moral value of the long-term consequences of having achieved that goal. (The moral value of trying to achieve a particular goal would then be determined by referring to the agent's beliefs and intentions at the time of her action, as well as to other important facts bearing on the context of her action.) But what if the goal itself is morally blameworthy? Would we still call the agent courageous if she, confronting her fears, tries to achieve a despicable goal? The goal of the person who saved little Adolf was to save a helpless and innocent child, not to help bringing about the Holocaust, and since the goal of saving an innocent child is considered a good one, we readily conclude that the agent was courageous in facing the dangers involved. But what if the agent's goal had been to achieve personal fame for herself by first setting a house on fire and then, confronting her fears of personal transience, running into the flames to save some innocent child? Would we still call that agent courageous?

This question, however, presupposes that courage must be a *moral* virtue, and that villains cannot be courageous. Now, I believe this position would complicate matters unnecessarily. For one thing, we would be deprived of the possibility to distinguish between those villains who, in addition to being villains, act like cowards (bullying only defenceless people whom they need not fear), and those who do not. To the extent that we think of courage as a certain psychological disposition of the agent (to be able to confront fear), it seems only reasonable to say that similar dispositions should be judged similarly, and that courage is courage regardless of the goals involved. If soldier *A* is courageous as he makes a rush over a field under heavy fire in order to rescue a wounded comrade, then soldier *B* is also courageous as he, under similar conditions, rescues a fellow soldier. Likewise, if *A* is courageous in single-handedly attacking an enemy stronghold, then *B* is also courageous when he, under similar conditions, attacks an enemy position. And this would hold, even if *A* fights for a tyrannical and expansionist dictator and *B* fights on the side of democracy and liberty. The villain robbing trains may confront the Pinkerton detectives with courage. And the soldier fighting for what he believes is a just cause could be courageous even if it turns out in the end that he was mistaken about the cause for which he endangered his life. As John F. Kennedy remarked:

> Must men conscientiously risk their careers only for principles which hindsight declares to be correct, in order for posterity to honor them for their valor? I think not. Surely in the United States of America, where brother once fought against brother, we did not judge a man's bravery under fire by examining the banner under which he fought. (Kennedy, p. 240.)

Consequently, I will differ from Douglas Walton, who seems to hold that our evaluation of the goodness of the agent's goal of action should determine our assessment of whether or not the agent's action deserves to be called "courageous". However, Walton is not very clear about what is most important in this context: that the agent *believes* that she is acting for a good cause, or that she believes this and is *justified* in so believing.

On the one hand, Walton claims that "[t]o be truly courageous, the act must be carried out with intentions that are of moral worth" (p. 95). Moreover, he adds that the agent's action "must have been done for a justifiably worthwhile end that ... has genuine moral significance as a virtuous end" (ibid.). This seems to imply an "objective" interpretation of the courageous action, according to which it does not suffice that the agent herself believes it to be justified, but that it must really *be* justified. Not just any intention will do, but only intentions that are of "moral worth".

On the other hand, in his reflections on the evaluation of actions of the historical past, Walton argues that "[s]ometimes the proper evaluation of such acts is very difficult to reconstruct and may involve virtually a whole biographical saga, taking into account the moral beliefs and deliberations of the agent" (p. 117). Here Walton's focus is on the subjective aspects of courageous agency, namely, the contents of the agent's mind at the time of her action. This subjectivist conception of courage is reinforced, when Walton goes on to claim that "the real merit of an act of courage is that it shows the good intentions of the agent at the time and his commitment to those intentions" (p. 182).

But then the picture is muddled again, as Walton goes on to argue, on one and the same page, both that "a courageous act is always directed toward a good end" and that "an act of courage is justified primarily by its intentions" (p. 189). What are we to make of this? The first proposition, that a courageous act is always directed toward a good end, does not refer to any agent's beliefs. As it stands, it permits the interpretation that a good end should be distinguished from an end which an agent *believes* to be good, and that it is only ends of the first kind that may confer the label "courageous" on an action. This would amount to an objectivist account of the justification of courage. The second proposition, however, clearly ties the issue of justification to the agent's intentions, and hence to what she believes is a good end. Accordingly, this would constitute a subjectivist account of the justification of courage.

Likewise, from Walton's discussion of the case of Rommel, it seems as if he would favour a subjectivist account, but then he introduces provisions that seem to point in the objectivist direction. German Field-Marshal Erwin Rommel is an interesting case indeed. On the one hand, he has been generally esteemed as a highly competent and professional soldier, respected as a fair and fearless opponent also by enemy officers. On the other hand, although not a Nazi himself, Rommel was one of Hitler's generals, and his bravery and strategic genius served that same Nazi empire which organized the Holocaust and brought war and destruction on an unprecedented scale to the world. Now, could it be appropriate to apply the term "courageous" to any action performed by Rommel, given the character of the state for which he was fighting? Walton initially adopts the subjectivist approach:

> What was Rommel's purpose or end in conducting the African campaign in the way he did? The question is not what the actual consequences of his conduct were, but how he perceived the possible consequences at the time.... If we ask why Rommel acted in a particular way during a particular engagement, his end may have been to seize the initiative, to shorten his supply lines, or whatever. But in attempting to evaluate the real worth of the end he had in view, that information is not directly helpful. We need to know whether, in pursuing all these limited ends, he was still thinking that his efforts were helping his country in a worthy struggle or if he had begun to realize the corruption and evil that had taken hold in Germany. (Walton, p. 125.)

The paradox of this subjectivist approach is, however, that it presupposes an objectivist evaluative framework. Walton aims at evaluating "the real worth" of Rommel's end, and he asks whether Rommel might have begun to realize the evil features of the state he was fighting for, which, of course, implies that Rommel could have been wrong about his perceived ends, i.e., to the extent that he did *not* realize the true nature of the Nazi state. Moreover, the idea that we might be wrong about the goodness of our ends is defended explicitly by Walton, immediately after his discussion of the Rommel case:

> We have seen ... that there is always an element of moral luck and riskiness in taking a stand. Despite your best efforts to take the most plausible moral position, it could become clearer later that your position cannot be justified. (Walton, p. 125.)

However, no matter whether the subjectivist or the objectivist account is correct, Walton's discussion is problematic at a more fundamental level, as it seems to confuse the issue of *defining* the term "courage" with the issue of *justifying* courageous acts. The reason for this confusion is, of course, an assumption that a courageous act by definition must be a morally justified act. But there is no reason why we should make this assumption. As von Wright notes,

> To be courageous is necessarily a good thing for the brave man himself, when he is facing danger – although, of course, what courage does to help him may become counteracted by other things which work against him. Courage can also be of the greatest importance to action which is done for the sake of others, *e.g.* in battle or when saving our neighbour from disaster. But whether a man's courage is or is not useful in the service of the good of others, depends upon the attitude which he happens to take to this good, or is compelled to take by external circumstances, such as threat of punishment if he flies. The courage which burglars or robbers display, can be much to the detriment of their neighbour's welfare. The value of courage from a 'social' point of view is therefore accidental; it depends upon the attitude, which the brave man happens to take to his fellow-humans. (von Wright, p. 153.)

Against this view, Philippa Foot has argued that not all daring actions deserve to be called "courageous". Foot wants to preserve a moral content in the concept of courage which would make it inappropriate to call villains courageous, although they go about their deeds in a fearless manner:

> Suppose for instance that a sordid murder were in question, say a murder done for gain or to get an inconvenient person out of the way, but that this murder had to be done in alarming circumstances or in the face of real danger; should we be happy to say that such an action was an act of courage or a courageous act? Did the murderer, who certainly acted boldly, or with intrepidity, if he did the murder, also act courageously?... There is no doubt that the murderer who murdered for gain was *not a coward*: he did not have a second moral defect which another villain might have had…. It does not follow, however, that an act of villainy can be courageous; we are inclined to say that it 'took courage', and yet it

seems wrong to think of courage as equally connected with good actions and bad. (Foot, pp. 15–16.)

However, we must ask ourselves whether our reluctance to call villains courageous just because they are villains is not based on a misunderstanding of what the concept of courage does or does not permit. It is understandable that we are not eager to call agents and actions that we dislike courageous, since "courageous" *is* a term of praise – in this Foot is right – and we are not disposed to lavish praise on people we despise. But although "courageous" is a term of praise, it does not follow that it is a term of *moral* praise. A courageous person is someone who gets things done, even in the face of adversity. Courage fortifies the agent and makes it possible for her to achieve in a way that cowards are not capable of. What we admire in the courageous agent is her ability to perform even under difficult psychological circumstances. But our admiration for her capacity to perform does not necessarily extend to an admiration of her goals or even of herself as a person. (Think of Alexander the Great or Richard III, for instance. They are undoubtedly courageous, but, from a moral point of view, they are also flawed by character traits such as vanity and ruthlessness.) Hence, although courage constitutes a *prudential value* (a good that enhances our capacity for successful agency), it is not necessarily a *moral value*. Hence, to call a villain courageous does not have the moral implications that Foot thinks and that makes her reject von Wright's argument.

Likewise, we should note that even if the agent in one context of action displays a courage that deserves moral praise, we should not infer that she will do the morally right thing in another context of action. An agent may on one occasion courageously defend a friend who is the innocent victim of an enraged mob. On another occasion the same agent may, with equal courage, attack an innocent person who is protected by a large number of armed men. Cases like this are likely to trouble us, since we often want the world to be a place of moral regularity and predictability, that is, a place where heroes are always heroes, and crooks are always crooks. That is why we have certain difficulties dealing with persons who are morally ambiguous, such as SS officers who care about animals and children, or human rights activists who embezzle humanitarian relief funds:

> We read of people doing what seems splendid; the sort of action that seems to call for an exceptional level of, say, courage or generosity. And then we learn about them that they have also done something morally repellent and we are surprised and often puzzled.... [T]he agent who dashed into the burning building and saved a stranger turns out to be a rapist; the one who has given a huge proportion of his income to the homeless turns out to be someone whose lies are keeping an innocent person in gaol. And we are surprised and puzzled: how could they be so splendid in the one instance and so despicable in another, we wonder? (Hursthouse, p. 155.)

As I have made clear above, my solution to the problem caused by the moral ambiguity of agents is simply to reject the idea that courage has any necessary relation to morality. Courage *may* serve morality, but this is not a matter of logical or empirical necessity.

Moreover, the idea that courage as a virtue should be analysed and understood independently of any assumptions regarding its necessary moral goodness can be further substantiated by reflecting on what would be involved in reforming a courageous Nazi:

> Consider what would be involved ... in the moral re-education of such a Nazi: there were many vices that he had to unlearn, many virtues which he had to learn. Humility and charity would be in most ways, if not quite in every way, new to him. But it is crucial that he would not have to unlearn or relearn what he knew about avoiding both cowardice and intemperate rashness in the face of harm and danger.... To deny that that kind of Nazi was courageous or that his courage was a virtue obliterates the distinction between what required moral re-education in such a person and what did not. (MacIntyre, p. 180.)

But what of cases, such as those discussed earlier, of either leaving or remaining in a slum environment, of either continuing or ending one's use of drugs? What would be the courageous choice here? If we agree, as I suggested, that the more dangerous option is, respectively, to remain in the slum and to continue using drugs, then it seems only reasonable to claim that the agent opting for either of these two alternatives is also able to confront fear, e.g., the fear of dying from a drug overdose or being killed by a slum gang. Hence, although my intention in introducing these cases was to disconnect courage from any necessary connection to danger (the courageous alternatives being to leave the slum and to quit using drugs), I thereby also opened up another way in which the discarded options still could claim to be recognized as courageous. This is so, since I have defined "courage" in terms of "the ability to confront fear". Assuming that where there is danger there is likely to be fear, it would follow that to remain in the slum and to continue using drugs indeed are courageous, since these options are dangerous and hence involve the likelihood of the agent's having to confront fear. Assuming that the agent is indeed able to confront the fear in question, she would also be a courageous agent. Hence, *both* the person who quits the slum *and* the one who remains are courageous due to the different kinds of fear they will have to cope with. Likewise, *both* the person who abstains from drugs *and* the one who continues to use them would be courageous. Hence, it would seem that I could maintain my original position (that it is courageous to leave the slum and quit using drugs, but not courageous to remain in the slum and continue using drugs) only by tacitly assuming what I have just denied, namely, that the courageous act should have a goal that is worthy of praise.

However, this would be to misconstrue my argument. Most importantly, it would be to miss a central point in my definition of "courage", namely, that it is about *confronting* fear. To confront one's fear is different from just enduring it. It is about setting oneself to *do* something in spite of being afraid. The person who works herself out of a slum environment is not content with just enduring a miserable life. She tries to do something to improve her lot by her own efforts. Likewise, the person who quits using drugs is not content to be a prisoner of her addiction and to adjust her life to the cravings of her poisoned brain. She does something to regain control over her life. This is what confronting is all about: to *act* in pursuit of a goal in spite of the fears one may have regarding failure or loss of life and health. And this is why it is courageous to break away from the slum rather than to endure it, and to quit using drugs rather than to give in to one's drug addiction.

The person who chooses to remain in the slum or to continue to use drugs may indeed fear for her life. But she does *not* confront her fear. She passively accepts the dangers involved in her way of life. She obviously does not like the situation she is in (why should she fear for her life if she did?), but this does not propel her into any action to change the conditions of her existence. Hence, there is no element of confronting fear here, but rather a sullen acceptance of fearful conditions of life.

Now, it could be argued that if she has chosen to remain in the slum and to continue using drugs, these *are* the goals she is pursuing, and so she is, after all, doing something. Hence there is no passivity on the part of the agent here. She only acts in a way different from the drug-rejecting and slum-quitting agent, that is all. And since they both show themselves able to confront fear, they are both courageous.

But there is a flaw in this argument. While the drug-rejecting slum-quitter fears what will happen if she is not successful in the pursuit of her goal, the drug-using slum-dweller on the contrary fears what will happen if she indeed succeeds in the pursuit of her goal, i.e., the goal of remaining a drug-using slum-dweller. Now, to be able to confront fear in the pursuit of one's goal (the definition of "courage" defended here) means that fear is to be overcome with the intention that one should successfully achieve one's goal. The fear is something that stands in the way of the agent's pursuit of her goal, not a consequence of her successfully attaining that goal. Hence, while the drug-rejecting slum-quitter indeed has to confront the fear of failure, the drug-using slum-dweller is rather in the position of one who is confronting "the fear of success". However, this should count as an indication of deep irrationality (when one's goals have such a content that one has to fear for their successful realization), rather than as an indication of courage.

However, although courage presupposes the agent being able to confront fear, courage should not be confused with the *absence* of fear.

Rather, in cases of danger, courage is about acting appropriately *in spite of* being afraid. In the words of Georg Henrik von Wright:

> What does it mean that the courageous man has learnt to conquer his fear? It does *not* mean that he no longer feels fear when facing danger. The brave man is not necessarily 'fearless' in the sense that he knows no fear. Some courageous men may even feel fear intensely. (von Wright, p. 147.)

This is what is meant by confronting fear: not that the agent should be insensitive to risks and dangers, but rather that she possesses an ability to pursue her goals unhampered by her fears. A similar view of courage is taken by psychologist Stanley Rachman, who defines it as "persistence in the face of subjective and physical sensations of fear" (Rachman, p. 12). Courage requires that the agent can master her fears, not that she should be a stranger to them. To be a coward is, on the other hand, not just being afraid. The coward is *controlled* by his fear, while courage is about overcoming one's fear to such an extent that one does not lose hold of oneself as an agent. It is not about denying fear, however. Now, Shakespeare has Julius Caesar (act 2, scene 2) proclaim:

> Cowards die many times before their deaths;
> The valiant never taste of death but once.

One way of reading this is that cowards do not die as agents, that is, they give up themselves as self-controlling purposive beings, and succumb to the fears and the panic that reduce them to mere victims of external circumstances. What courage can do is to restore one's sense of autonomy even in cases of adversity. Indeed, autonomy implies that "[o]ne should avoid regarding oneself solely as a victim, even if one's external circumstances, genetic or environmental, may warrant such a description" (Gewirth, 1998, p. 114).

It is important to note here that I think of courage as a *relational* property, rather than an *essential* one. That is, I believe that an agent's courage should be analysed in relation to particular goals and actions of hers, not as a permanent trait of character of hers. Hence, a person might be courageous in one context, and controlled by fear in another. A similar point has been argued by Douglas Walton:

> The courageous act in itself ... can be an object of merit and commendation apart from the question of the character of the agent as a general disposition. (Walton, p. 182.) The value of courage is not exclusively a matter of personal merit. A man may, in his lifetime, perform only one courageous act, and many cowardly actions. It does not follow that he is a courageous man. It is the act that is courageous, most fundamentally .... (Walton, p. 184.)

A Sioux chief may be able to confront his fears as he leads his nation in war, and yet be a prey to anxiety and uncontrollable fear when forced to settle down alone in a city suburb, deprived of the natural and social context that he identifies with. Likewise, a tough and street-wise city kid may lose his nerve when left in the deep woods, in an environment which his experience has not prepared him for. However, the fact that an agent is not *always* courageous should not lead us to hold that she is *never* courageous. Courage can be gained and it can be lost. The person who was courageous yesterday, could be unable to confront her fears tomorrow. Likewise, the person who used to give in to her fears may turn out to be a future hero. Hence, when we say of a person P, that "P is courageous", we should understand this statement as referring to a particular situation S at a particular time T, and a particular goal G: "P is courageous in S at T regarding G". Of course, it is possible to conceive of a person of whom this proposition would be true at all times, in all situations, and for all of her goals. But we should not make it a matter of definition that the courageous agent could never be anything but courageous.

This analysis seems to be in agreement with Aristotle's view of courage and other virtues of character as *dispositions* to be inculcated by habit and training, not natural faculties like seeing and hearing. They are "engendered in us neither *by* nor *contrary to* nature; we are constituted by nature to receive them, but their full development in us is due to habit" (Aristotle, 1103a14–b1, p. 91; see also 1104a33–b20, p. 95 and 1105b19–1106a13, pp. 98–99).

It is also important not to conflate courage with rashness. Courage should reflect a choice on the part of the agent, and not just express a fearless lack of self-control. This is important, since I want to be able to discuss courage in terms of actions, that is, as controlled and purposive behaviour, and not just as reflexes beyond the subject's control. Hence, I will follow Aristotle in assuming that the person who is afraid of nothing "would be a maniac or insensate" and that "[t]he man who exceeds in confidence about things that are fearful is rash" (Aristotle, 1115b19–1116a6, p. 129). Accordingly, the courageous person is not someone who *enjoys* fearful conditions. On the contrary, the value of courage is that it enables the agent to master circumstances which she does *not* enjoy, but which have to be endured if the agent is to be successful in the pursuit of her goals. As Rosalind Hursthouse points out:

> [W]hat seems beyond dispute is that someone who wants to risk and endure frightful pain or death, and enjoys doing so, is not thereby courageous but a masochist, or a daredevil maniac. Even when the courageous are not acting contrary to an inclination to run away or preserve themselves, they are not, in any ordinary sense, 'doing what they want to do' and thereby reaping the pleasure of satisfied desire. (Hursthouse, p. 96.)

CHAPTER 3

The Courage of Creativity

Now, courage should be understood as a complex virtue, including two distinct forms, related to the two types of fear discussed above. Hence, we can talk of the *courage of creativity*, which is the ability to confront the fear of failure, this ability being directed by the agent's will to achieve, as well as the *courage of conviction*, which is the ability to confront the fear of personal transience, this ability being directed by the agent's sense of moral responsibility.

The *courage of creativity* is related to a person's conception of herself as an agent with purposes of her own. It involves being inventive and persistent in overcoming obstacles and adversities in the pursuit of one's goals. It also involves being independent in the choice of these goals, rather than passively acquiescing in social conventions or in the expectations of others. This does not, of course, mean that the agent should make it a virtue to frustrate other people's expectations. But it is important that the goals she is trying to realize indeed are *her* goals. They need not be hers only, but the reason for the agent's pursuit of them should be that *she* finds it important from *her* personal point of view to achieve them. Hence, a certain goal may well originate in the plans and projects of another person, but in order for it to be independently adopted by the agent she should herself desire its accomplishment for reasons of her own.

It is important to note here that the courage of creativity supports the *personal* good of the agent, furthering her long-term plans (e.g., for a certain career or way of life) as well as her more immediate projects (e.g., learning to swim or delivering a lecture). By saying that the courage of creativity supports the agent's personal good, I also intend the implication that the focus here is not on the universal good of mankind or any such impersonal or other-regarding conception of the good. This is not the courage of the person who willingly risks her life for her country, but rather the courage of the person who is prepared to endure hardship and adversity to secure for herself the kind of life she wants to have. To have a conception of one's personal good is to have at least some idea of what one's life would be like at its best, and to apply that idea to one's long-term projects as well as to one's particular actions. There is plenty of room for individual variation here, and a person's idea of her good is likely to be influenced, at least to some extent, by values and traditions specific to her time and society. (It should be noted, however, that as the courage of creativity promotes an independent assessment of goals, the perfectly courageous agent will not simply be a product of her culture and time, but capable of evaluating her goals from a personal point of view.)

Now, an agent's promotion of her personal good requires that she is resourceful and persistent in her efforts to overcome difficulties and adversities. The courage of creativity provides the agent with the psychological strength necessary for her to be successful in her endeavours. It also implies an attitude of determination in the face of obstacles, according to which the agent, whenever she suffers a setback, instead of giving up or starting to complain about how bad things are, will tell herself, "This is the material out of which I will make something good." The person who possesses the courage of creativity never forgets that she is an *agent*, and that she has a personal responsibility for making the most of her life, regardless of the circumstances she finds herself in.

The courage of creativity includes what Daniel Putnam has labelled "psychological courage", which he distinguishes from the "physical courage" involved in overcoming a fear of death or physical harm, as well as the "moral courage" of maintaining one's moral integrity and overcoming the fear of social rejection, when the latter is an expected consequence of making one's views public. Psychological courage, according to Putnam, is about overcoming a fear that centres around a loss of psychological stability. And as the courage of creativity counteracts the fear of failure, by reminding the agent of the possibility of turning despair into constructive agency, it also counteracts the fear of losing control:

I speak of the courage it takes to face our irrational fears and anxieties, those passions which, in Spinoza's terms, hold us in bondage. These can range from habits and compulsions to phobias. Aristotle would have classified many of these under lack of temperance. A drinking habit or an irrational fear of open spaces reflects a lack of proper balance regarding the pleasures of life. But facing and working through these habits or anxieties can involve courage for several reasons. First, to admit the problem is to face the possibility of being stigmatized by society. In this sense psychological courage has some similarities to moral courage. Second, a great deal of pain, physical and psychological, can be involved in confronting the anxiety or changing the habit, and the individual knows this beforehand. Third, and most significant to this form of courage, the stability of the psyche itself is threatened (or perceived to be threatened) by the process of coping with the problem. (Putnam, p. 2.)

Now, from a psychological point of view, the courage of creativity and the agent's determination to make the most of her lot, even when success does not seem to be within immediate reach, could be said to reflect an *agency-related optimism*. This agency-related optimism expresses itself in the agent's capacity for *positive planning*. In positive planning we concentrate on how to succeed in our endeavours, rather than on how to avoid failure. We aim at making the most of our goals and projects, given the opportunities at hand, rather than simply minimizing risks. This does not mean that we turn a blind eye to the possibility of failure, but we do not allow that possibility to prevent us from going ahead. We plan for success, not for failure, and as we encounter obstacles we will do our best to overcome them there and then, but the mere possibility of failure should not deter us from trying to achieve. Positive planning is likely to develop the agent's confidence in her powers of agency, focusing on what she in fact can do, rather than on what she is unable to do. Perhaps this is what Aristotle had in mind when he contrasted the confidence of the courageous man with the despondency of the coward, concluding that "confidence is the mark of optimism" (Aristotle, 1115b19–1116a6, p. 129).

Positive planning derives from a more general principle which we may label *the principle of constructive creativity*. This principle simply prescribes that we should always try to make the most of things, in terms of ends as well as means, given the opportunities at hand. The strength of the principle lies in its very generality of application. Regardless of whether or not the situation at hand fulfils our expectations or hopes, regardless of whether or not our previous efforts to realize our goals have been successful, and regardless of whether or not our prospects for the future look bright, the principle of constructive creativity enjoins us to make the most of things as they are here and now. Hence, adherence to this principle will make us less intimidated by the prospect of failure, as it encourages us to move on, to the best of our ability, rather than brooding on what has gone wrong. The fact that a particular plan of ours has failed does not entail that we should give up or assume a pessimistic view of ourselves as agents. On the contrary, we should review the situation at hand, examining the possibilities it offers, and see whether there is another way to accomplish the plan that failed, or whether there are other goals of worth that we should try to realize instead. We are not required to be always successful in our purpose-fulfilment, but we are required to make a responsible use of the opportunities at hand, even if they may look meagre. (A somewhat similar principle of action is advanced by Douglas Walton, who stresses the value of "taking advantage of the circumstances", which involves "the quick perception or sizing up of a situation and the ability to exploit quickly changing circumstances without losing one's head" (p. 129).)

Hence, the principle of constructive creativity makes it possible to include in the description of the courage of creativity some of the valuable features that are thought of as belonging to the virtue of patience. Eamonn Callan, for instance, argues that what is sometimes believed to be a lack of courage should be better understood as a lack of patience. Callan gives us an example of a man who grows blind in the prime of his life, and who cannot find it in himself to accommodate to his new situation. Although he is otherwise healthy, prosperous, and surrounded by people whom he loves and who love him, he remains in the grip of despair and anger brought on by his blindness. Now, Callan continues, it could be argued that the man's inability to accept his lot is due to a lack of fortitude, i.e., the courage to remain unperturbed in the face of pain. But this will not do as an explanation of the man's state of mind, according to Callan:

> Attributing a lack of fortitude mislocates the problem because it suggests that the difficulty has to do with the way the man bears his suffering when in truth it has more to do [with] why he suffers so much in the first place. If he could grow to accept the good that is available, he would not suffer so much in his blindness, and hence the need for fortitude would not be so great. The blind man in my story has no patience for the moral task his blindness has set him, and no amount of courage or fortitude can compensate for the absence of that virtue. (Callan, p. 526.)

But "to accept the good that is available" is exactly the position encouraged by the principle of constructive creativity, although it implies more than just a passive acceptance. Like patience, this principle requires of us that we refrain from brooding and sulking over the bad deal that we have been given, and that we take a constructive view of what can be achieved, given our capabilities and the opportunities at hand. And this is indeed a form of courage, but not the courage of stoic endurance that Callan seems to have in mind. Instead it is the courage of being able to confront one's fear of failure, and have another try at realizing a good life for oneself.

Adherence to the principle of constructive creativity and the practice of positive planning entailed by that principle will fortify the agent against the impact of failures and reversals. Hence, the constructively creative agent will function as Daniel Goleman's optimistic insurance salesman in his example of two different reactions to the experience of being repeatedly rejected by potential customers:

> Each no a salesperson gets is a small defeat. The emotional reaction to that defeat is crucial to the ability to marshal enough motivation to continue. As the noes mount up, morale can deteriorate, making

it harder and harder to pick up the phone for the next call. Such rejection is especially hard to take for a pessimist, who interprets it as meaning, "I'm a failure at this; I'll never make a sale" – an interpretation that is sure to trigger apathy and defeatism, if not depression. Optimists, on the other hand, tell themselves, "I'm using the wrong approach," or "That last person was just in a bad mood." By seeing not themselves but something in the situation as the reason for their failure, they can change their approach in the next call. While the pessimist's mental set leads to despair, the optimist's spawns hope. (Goleman, p. 101.)

Conceptually, positive planning seems to presuppose an attitude that we may call *positive possibilism*, and which is also implied by the principle of constructive creativity. The content of this attitude is that a good outcome is indeed possible, whether we speak of a complete life or a particular goal of action. (Positive possibilism does not imply, however, that all actions carry the same potential for success. It entails that success is possible, but we still have to apply our powers of judgement to find out which line of action is most likely to bring about the desired outcome.)

Positive possibilism may be supported by a related attitude, which we may call *positive actualism*. This attitude maintains simply that the way things are is not the worst possible. It might appear to be a rather timid stand to take for a view which aspires to be called "positive". But we should note that positive actualism does not rule out a more cheerful perspective on the world. It is perfectly consistent with this attitude to hold that this is the best of all conceivable worlds. The only thing that positive actualism will not accept is the deep pessimistic view that the way things are is the worst possible. And it is the moderate character of this claim that is the greatest asset of positive actualism, compared to other forms of optimism. While it is rather easy to falsify the idea that this is the best of all conceivable worlds simply by pointing to the occurrence of evil and misery, it is much more difficult to make a plausible argument to the effect that this is the worst state of affairs possible. With a little imagination we may easily conclude that although we are not perfectly happy, things could be worse, and sometimes much worse, than they actually are. And as this way of thinking tends to weaken our disposition to complain about our lot, we may come to take a more hopeful view of our possibilities for successful action. Hence, positive actualism supports positive possibilism.

More recently, Nicholas Rescher has defended the idea of *attitudinal optimism*, which, unlike factual optimism, "is not a matter of a cognitively based conviction regarding how things will comport themselves in the world, but represents a praxis-geared posture of hopeful belief" (Rescher, p. 98). Attitudinal optimism advocates that in the absence of contrary information we should hope for the best. "It inserts itself into the gaps that arise where established facts are insufficient or indecisive, neither resting on the facts of the matter, nor defying them" (Rescher, p. 99). And, as Rescher points out, attitudinal optimism may well have a pragmatic value even when its hopes are not fulfilled, since it motivates us to make efforts to improve things that we otherwise would not undertake. Now, the agency-related optimism of positive planning inherent in the courage of creativity is similar to Rescher's attitudinal optimism in that it is indeed "praxis-geared", focusing on what to *do* given one's goals and the opportunities at hand. But whereas Rescher's attitudinal optimism rests on "hopeful belief", the agency-related optimism of positive planning does not hope for anything. It simply asserts that we should plan for success, not for failure. Hence, it is more of a prescription than a belief.

Now, what would make an agent adopt this kind of prescription if she is not already an agency-related optimist? I have committed myself to the view that it is the will to achieve that motivates the agent to develop in herself the courage of creativity. If it were not for the projects that we want to realize, the careers that we strive for, the enjoyments that we want to experience, in short, if it were not for the lives that we want to lead, we would indeed have no reason to try to overcome difficulties and adversities. However, as long as we can conceive of ends and states of affairs that we want to realize, and as long as we can conceive of ourselves as deriving some sense of fulfilment or satisfaction from their realization, we will be motivated to involve ourselves in positive planning in accordance with the principle of constructive creativity. (What seems to happen to people that suffer from depression is that they lose all interest in their own lives as well as the world around them, thereby also losing the ability to formulate goals that might inspire their agency. The loss of the will to achieve then further reinforces the lack of courage and leaves the agent in a state of passivity. In fact, the agent here seems to give up her very identity as an agent, and turn herself into a vegetative state of existence.)

We are born with a curiosity that makes us reach out for the world, experiencing it, exploring it, and conquering it. If our curiosity is thwarted, by the rigidity or timidity of our social environment or by unpleasant personal experiences, we may well fail to develop the courage of creativity, or we may develop it only to a certain level. But in the absence of such limiting experiences, our curiosity will mature to become a selective instrument, driving us on to explore particular aspects of the world, according to our personal predilections. And so this explorative venture will manifest itself in goals of action, whether in the form of immediate purposes to be fulfilled (preparing an exquisite Italian meal) or in the form of long-term projects (becoming an archaeologist of world renown). All these purposes and projects will require the ability to confront the fear of failure, and the very will to achieve them will provide the agent with the motivation initially necessary to go ahead and confront that fear. And as the agent inculcates in herself the habit of positive planning, thereby improving her capacity for successful agency, her confidence in her powers of agency will increase and that confidence will in turn reinforce her willingness and ability to confront her fear of failure.

In the process the agent may have to make difficult and painful decisions, such as quitting a job that tends to hamper her pursuit of a good life, or ending a frustrating love-affair to protect her self-esteem from dropping to a level so low that it threatens her very capacity for successful agency. In all these difficult and painful decisions the agent will need to mobilize a courage of creativity. So how does she manage to mobilize that courage in the first place?

The starting-point is, I believe, the agent's awareness that her life is not as good as it should and could be, and that it is up to her to do something to improve her lot. The next step is to ascertain what has to be done to realize the desired improvement, and what the cost will be to herself of making the necessary changes in her circumstances. The final move is for the agent to initiate an appropriate set of actions that will bring about these changes, without being deflected from her purpose by the pain and the sense of insecurity and vulnerability inherent in all new beginnings. As she manages to persist in her pursuit (finding a new job, making new friends, moving to another city, acquiring new skills, and so on) she will become more and more confident in her powers of agency. That initial sparkle of courage which originally made her question the basic conditions of her life has now grown into a fully developed courage of creativity which allows her to explore more fully what the world has to offer.

Now, in the absence of the agency-related optimism inherent in the courage of creativity we would find it hard to achieve our projects, since we might be absorbed by the *negative planning* emanating from the fear of failure, obsessively searching for guarantees that nothing will go wrong. If positive planning focuses on how to be successful, negative planning focuses on how to avoid risk and failure. This focus on risk-aversion in negative planning reinforces rather than mitigates the agent's fear of failure, as it constantly reminds her of the possibility that something might go wrong, and that she has to protect herself against the harmful effects of failure. And as the agent sets out to prevent failure and protect herself from risk, negative planning will point to all the possible flaws in her protective measures. Hence, she will be even more exposed to feelings of vulnerability, as her very efforts to react to the promptings of negative planning will be mercilessly judged from the perspective of negative planning. Consequently, the agent engaging in negative planning will be driven into a negative spiral of ever-increasing despair regarding her possibilities for successful action, losing all confidence in her powers of agency along the way. She will occupy herself with fending off disaster rather than with expanding her capacity for successful agency.

It is interesting to note in this context that recent work in the field of cognitive psychology seems to be able to trace a connection between negative representations of the world and the occurrence of panic attacks:

[T]here is evidence that panic patients have a higher frequency of the cognitions that lend themselves to catastrophic misinterpretations. They are more likely to experience thoughts of impending loss of control, loss of consciousness, heart attack, and so on than are people who have anxiety that is not associated with a panic experience.... Experimental studies have shown that panic patients are significantly more likely to interpret their bodily sensations in a mistaken and catastrophic manner than are people who do not experience panic attacks. Furthermore, there are early indications that if a catastrophic misinterpretation is activated, the probability of experiencing a panic is significantly increased. (Rachman, p. 128.)

Likewise, people liable to depressive illness tend to "over-estimate the significance and the probabilities of unpleasant events, and play down the value of positive events, or fail even to perceive that they are positive" (Rachman, p. 133). Hence, just as positive planners can be described as adherents of the principle of constructive creativity, it might be appropriate to describe negative planners as adherents of *the principle of destructive creativity*. This principle, if it were to be articulated in explicit terms, enjoins us to take the most dismal view possible of the situation at hand, and to act accordingly. It guides our creative powers down the path of pessimism, making us see problems, obstacles, dangers, and threats which nobody else would perceive. Needless to say, not many people would openly and explicitly subscribe to such a principle, but this does not mean that the principle does not have any followers. Adherents of the principle of destructive creativity are those who engage their powers of imagination to find problems rather than solutions, who remember well all the things that have gone wrong in the past, who are unable to convince themselves that things might work out fine in the future, and who are in a constant fear that something bad is about to happen, occupying themselves with emergency plans to escape an impending disaster. We should note, however, that also people who are normally positive planners may occasionally fall prey to the principle of destructive creativity, due to the impact of, for instance, an unexpected loss or some other traumatic experience.

The Persian king Xerxes seems to have been acutely aware of the paralysing effects of negative planning. According to Herodotus, Xerxes was warned by his uncle Artabanus that his intention to subdue the Greeks might end in failure (which it eventually also did). Xerxes, however, criticized Artabanus for being obsessed with what could go wrong:

> But this I say, fear not everything, nor take account of all alike; for if on whatever occasion befal [sic] you were minded to take everything alike into account, you would never do anything; better it is to suffer half the dreaded ill by facing all with a stout heart, rather than to fear all chances and so suffer nought.... It is they, then, who have the will to act that do oftenest win the prizes, not, truly, they that palter and take account of all chances. (Herodotus, book vii, § 50; p. 365.)

Given Xerxes' actual failure, his rejection of timidity and negative planning may seem to be less than persuasive. But we should note that Xerxes' failure as a military strategist did not emanate from his refusal to endorse negative planning, but rather from a certain rashness on his part. The perfectly sound idea that we should not let ourselves be swamped by the possibility of failure does not entail the unsound conclusion that we need not care at all about the feasibility of our plans. Positive planning is still *planning*, implying a careful selection of means appropriate to our chosen ends.

Now, we should be aware that people are sometimes encouraged to develop patterns of negative planning. This is particularly evident in the preoccupation with health in the modern industrialized world, which tends to move from a prudent concern for nutritious food and exercise, to a more alarmist stage where we are reminded of the possible dangers of almost everything in our environment. As media try to exploit people's fears, a "risk epidemic" spreads:

> Newspapers, journals, TV-channels and movies that can trigger anxiety and thrills, obviously get high circulation and attendance rates. Supported by advertisements from the "anxiety industry", media convey horrifying descriptions of the threats from ebola

virus, flesh-eating germs, food poisoning and various "neglectful" life-styles. Bad news from epidemiologists, health promoters and public health agencies have seemingly open, and often uncritical, channels to the public. (Førde, p. 1156.)

As a consequence, people come to identify health with risk evasion. However, this implies a negative analysis of the concept of health, in terms of the absence of disease and death. It leaves out a wider conception of health, as self-realization, coping, psycho-physical functioning, or general well-being, which cannot be had without the agent being prepared to take some risks:

> The problem is that an extensive and dogmatic healthy life-style easily grows into general risk aversion and risk intolerance, which in turn may harm some of those other elements of the expanded health concept. A growing intolerance to risks and uncertainty is hardly the best basis for self-realisation and coping as long as uncertainty, unpredictability and risk are an inherent part of any human life that is worth living. A person obsessed with risk aversion is socially impaired and although it may sometimes look otherwise, the completely controlled, risk-free life and society has few, if any, open supporters. (Førde, p. 1157.)

The agent who possesses the courage of creativity, although she is not a gambler (at least not necessarily), is determined to resist the fear of failure, and when failure occurs she takes it as an encouragement to renew her efforts to achieve. This could be instructively contrasted with the behaviour of people who lack the agency-related optimism and the corresponding courage of creativity. These people will find themselves paralysed by their fear of failure and their constant need to reassure themselves that things will work out well. If we think of people who suffer from nervous illnesses and deep anxieties, and who need to assure themselves repeatedly that they have acted correctly (to see for themselves one more time that the oven is switched off, the door locked, the letter safely dropped in the mailbox, and so on), it will seem fairly obvious that they have succumbed to the fear of failure, and that they are in desperate need of courage.

Moreover, speaking of people who succumb to the fear of failure and who devote their lives to minimizing risks, we should note that an exaggerated focus on risks and negative expectations in general may result in depressive illness. Daniel Goleman suggests, in a discussion of the causes of a depressive tendency, that in addition to the genetic factor, "some of that tendency seems due to reversible, pessimistic habits of thought that predispose children to react to life's small defeats – a bad grade, arguments with parents, a social rejection – by becoming depressed" (Goleman, p. 275).

Hence, the courage of creativity is also a powerful instrument in the conquest of freedom, namely the freedom from a destructive and paralysing fear that otherwise may not only cloud an agent's judgement but also deprive her of confidence, this in turn "leading to destruction of that natural zest and appetite for possible things upon which all happiness, whether of men or animals, ultimately depends" (Russell, p. 13).

To the extent that the agent is successful in her plans and projects, her courage is likely to be reinforced, and she may go on to adopt new goals of action, expanding her abilities as she goes along. This is the dynamic aspect of the good life as agency-related capacity-fulfilment that Alan Gewirth has described as "additive well-being", that is, well-being viewed as a capacity to add to one's capabilities of action. As a result of the agent's critical reflection on her purposes and her learning from experience,

> additive well-being also involves acting on purposes that expand and deepen one's horizons of values and that not only reflect more authentically who one is but also transform who one is. It includes such virtues as being open to new experiences, new challenges, and new values, both personal and social. It also involves taking pleasure in these ranges of experience and value. In these ways one's self-fulfillment is also a self-expansion, but with all the risks inherent in the operational aspect of reason. (Gewirth, 1998, p. 123.)

What this dynamic factor may imply in practice can be gathered from Benjamin Franklin's description of how he applied himself to learning foreign languages:

> I had begun in 1733 to study languages. I soon made myself so much a master of the French as to be able to read the books with ease. I then undertook the Italian. I afterward with a little painstaking acquired as much of the Spanish as to read their books also. I have already mentioned that I had only one year's instruction in a Latin school, and that when very young, after which I neglected that language entirely. But when I had attained an acquaintance with the French, Italian, and Spanish, I was surprised to find, on looking over a Latin Testament, that I understood so much more of that language than I had imagined; which encouraged me to apply myself again to the study of it; and I met with the more success, as those preceding languages had greatly smoothed my way. (Tamarin, p. 71.)

The beneficial aspects of the courage of creativity are likely to include not only an increase in the agent's powers of agency, but also a strengthening of will of those in the agent's environment who depend on her. Isaiah Berlin's portrait of Franklin Delano Roosevelt provides an illuminating example here:

> He was one of the few statesmen in the twentieth or any other century who seemed to have no fear at all of the future. He believed in his own strength and ability to manage, and succeed, whatever happened. He believed in the capacity and loyalty of his lieutenants, so that he looked upon the future with a calm eye, as if to say 'Let it come, whatever it may be, it will all be grist to our great mill. We shall turn it all to benefit.' It was this, perhaps, more than any other quality, which drew men of very different outlooks to him. In a despondent world which appeared divided between wicked and fatally efficient fanatics marching to destroy, and bewildered populations on the run, unenthusiastic martyrs in a cause they could not define, he believed in his own ability, so long as he was at the controls, to stem this terrible tide. (Berlin, p. 26.)

To sum up, I believe we may safely conclude that the courage of creativity, with its insistence on constructive creativity and positive planning, is indeed essential to the good life of any human agent, as this good life should include the agent's capacity to be successful in her actions.

CHAPTER 4

The Courage of Conviction

While the courage of creativity is related to the agent's efforts to make the best of her personal life, the *courage of conviction* goes beyond the personal good of the agent, as it is constituted by the agent's ability to confront her fear of personal transience. The courage of conviction supports the *common* good rather than the agent's personal good, and it is directed by the agent's sense of moral responsibility.

The common good is the good of some community of which the agent perceives herself to be a member. The community in question could range from small-scale communities based on kinship or friendship, to ethnic, political, and religious communities, and even to very inclusive groups, such as the community of all agents or all sentient beings. It could be helpful in this context to think of the agent's various possible communal affiliations along the lines given by William Galston in his analysis of various dimensions of altruism:

> *Personal* altruism is directed toward individuals near at hand, such as family members and friends. *Communal* altruism is directed toward groups of individuals possessing some shared characteristics: members of an ethnic group, coreligionists, and fellow citizens, among others. *Cosmopolitan* altruism, by contrast, is directed toward the human race as a whole, and hence toward individuals to whom one has no special ties.... One could imagine a fourth variety – a *comprehensive* altruism directed toward all entities with interests. (Galston, p. 123.)

As for the contents of the good of a community, it will, of course, vary with the different purposes for which communities are formed and maintained (loyalty and support between friends, national independence, social justice, the implementation of God's will, and so forth). However, we should be aware that there is often a significant difference between positive and normative conceptions of the common good, that is, between what is actually believed within a particular community to be the common good of that community, and what *should* be regarded as the common good, given the rationally best justificatory argument. Hence, in the absence of such a justificatory argument, we cannot move from the premise that a certain conception of the common good is actually endorsed within a particular community, to the conclusion that this conception is valid and deserving of the respect and allegiance from the members of the community in question. (The contents of a morally justified common good will be discussed in chapter 6.)

Moreover, we should note that we may contribute to the common good not only by participating in collective undertakings, such as the military defence of our country, but also by assisting particular individuals who have their lives or other basic aspects of their well-being endangered (for instance, by a gang of street thugs). To the extent that the common good is conceived of as the maintenance of certain rights of individuals (whether in their capacity as citizens of a particular community, or as members of an imagined universal community of agents), such a significant contribution to the well-being of individual persons will also count as a contribution to the common good.

The sense of moral responsibility that motivates the agent to confront her fear of personal transience and to serve the common good should be understood against the background of human sociality. As people join together, whether for the sake of the intimate sharing involved in love and friendship, or for the purpose of promoting some particular goal that they have in common, they tend to develop feelings of mutuality. Now, these feelings of mutuality are likely to generate in the individual an identification with the interests and goals of the other members of her group. Their joys and sorrows become, at least to some extent (varying with the emotional intensity of group involvement and the temperament of the individual member) also her joys and sorrows. Accordingly, she will develop a sense of moral responsibility for the community as a whole, as well as for its individual members, perceiving herself as sharing with the other members certain interests, rights, and duties.

In the case of lovers it comes as no surprise that they tend to identify with each other's interests, even if not all lovers adopt the extreme self-effacement of Romeo, who, in response to Juliet's question, "Art thou not Romeo, and a Montague?", replies "Neither, fair maid, if either thee dislike" (*Romeo and Juliet*, Act 2, Scene 2). However, also in relationships that are not characterized by romantic overtones, there will develop feelings of mutuality from sharing some common purpose. Coming to rely on each other's support for the realization of their purpose, these feelings of mutuality will reinforce each participant's sense of responsibility regarding not only the purpose itself, but also regarding the well-being of the other participants. That is why Meriwether Lewis, on having completed his voyage to the American west coast in 1806, wrote to President Thomas Jefferson on behalf of his trusted partner in the expedition, William Clark, in order that he too should have his contribution to the common project recognized (spelling as in the original):

> With rispect to the exertions and services rendereed by that esteemable man Capt. William Clark in the course of [our] late voyage I cannot say too much; if sir any credit be due for the success of the arduous enterprise in which we have been mutually engaged, he is equally with myself entitled to your consideration and that of our common country. (Ambrose, p. 411.)

Now, it is important to note that feelings of mutuality may develop even in the absence of direct personal contact. People may experience themselves sharing political or religious projects with others of whom they have no personal knowledge, simply on account of their group identity (being members of the same nation, religious congregation, political party, and so on). This is why, for instance, a nation can be described as an "imagined" community:

> It is *imagined* because the members of even the smallest nation will never know most of their fellow-members, meet them, or even hear of them, yet in the minds of each lives the image of their

> communion.... Communities are to be distinguished, not by their falsity/genuineness, but by the style in which they are imagined. Javanese villagers have always known that they are connected to people they have never seen, but these ties were once imagined particularistically – as indefinitely stretchable nets of kinship and clientship. Until quite recently, the Javanese language had no word meaning the abstraction 'society'. (Anderson, p. 6.)

And sometimes individuals find it possible to imagine themselves as not only participating in a national project, but indeed in a project of much more inclusive dimensions, given a certain view of the ideals of their national community. The liberty at stake in the 1861–65 American Civil War conflict was sometimes given universal proportions. "I do feel that the liberty of the world is placed in our hands to defend, and if we are overcome then farewell to freedom", wrote a soldier in the 33rd Massachusetts in 1862. Likewise, a private in the 122nd Illinois was certain of the far-reaching implications of a Union victory: "if we succeed in establishing our Gov[ernment], *then you may look for European struggles for liberty*" (McPherson, pp. 112–113). A corporal in the 39th Ohio (who had been born in England) developed the same universalist theme in a letter to his wife, after having reenlisted for a second three-year term:

> If I do get hurt I want you to remember that it will be not only for my Country and my Children but for Liberty all over the World that I risked my life, for if Liberty should be crushed here, what hope would there be for the cause of Human Progress anywhere else? (McPherson, p. 113.)

Hence, the commitment to certain ideals developed within one kind of community may well extend beyond that community, given the potentially universalist qualities of the ideals in question (liberty, human rights), and given the willingness of agents to recognize the universalist qualities inherent in their ideals.

The Fear of Meaninglessness

As regards the fear of personal transience, this is not just about the fear of dying. It is also about the fear that one's life does not matter, and that its very transience makes it meaningless. Whatever happiness one might find is bound to be annihilated by one's death, and this fundamental condition of life threatens to deprive all one's projects of their significance. What is the point in trying to achieve, if in the end we are unable to hold on to our achievements? In the words of philosopher Irving Singer:

> Human beings seek a prior meaning in everything as a defense against doubts about the importance of anything, including man's existence. Though we see people expend a great deal of energy on matters of personal concern, we are also aware of human limitations. We know that we are mortal, living for fairly short periods, and that nothing we may do or feel can have a major influence upon the universe. There appears to be a disproportion between the seriousness with which men and women approach their multiple interests and the relative insignificance of these interests within the cosmos as a whole. If, however, the world itself pursues a goal toward which we all contribute, this basic disproportion would be resolved. What matters to us surely does matter if the course of reality includes it within some truly objective design. To affirm that there is a supreme meaning of life is to give the intellect an opportunity to escape the disquieting conclusion that *nothing* people do can possibly have more than slight importance. (Singer, 1996, p. 33.)

Sharing an important project and a common good with others (raising a family, solving scientific problems, building a nation, spreading the gospel) is a way to have one's life imbued with meaning. But it is important that you *do* something to promote the project in question. It does not suffice just to take an *interest* in it. It is by means of your agency that you prove yourself to be committed. As Robert Nozick has pointed out,

Meaning can be gained by linking with something of value. However, the nature of the linkage is important. I cannot give meaning to my life by saying I am linked to advancing justice in the world, where this means that I read the newspapers every day or week and thereby notice how justice and injustice fare. That is too trivial and too insubstantial a link. (Still, knowing external things and understanding how they are valuable may constitute a nontrivial link.) The greater the link, the closer, the more forceful, the more intense and extensive it is, the greater the meaning gotten. The tighter the connection with value, the greater the meaning. This tightness of connection means that you are interrelated with the value in a unified way; there is more of an organic unity between you and the value. Your connection with the value, then, is itself valuable; and meaning is gotten through such a valuable connection with value. (Nozick, p. 168.)

A similar conception of meaning, as the practical pursuit (and not only the desire for) objective value, is advocated by Susan Wolf, according to whom "meaningful lives are lives of active engagement in projects of worth" (Wolf, p. 209). Wolf also contributes the insightful remark that objectively worthy actions do not by themselves generate meaning. The agent has to be emotionally *involved* in what she does. A person may work as a doctor, "competently doing a socially valuable job", and yet fail to derive meaning from this "because she is not engaged by her work" (Wolf, p. 211).

Moreover, psychological research seems to confirm that, at least in times of war, there is a positive causal relation between being involved in socially meaningful work and being able to control one's fear of personal transience. Studies relating to the experiences of Londoners during the Blitz report that the German air raids did not cause any striking increase in neurotic illness. On the contrary,

> [i]n his wide-ranging survey of neurotic responses to air raids, Sir Aubrey Lewis, a doyen of British psychiatry, also remarked on the comparative invulnerability of firefighters and other people engaged in essential services. Moreover, the few men who required some assistance after exposure to heavy raids and were suffering from

exhaustion recovered rapidly after they had rested. Lewis suggests that engaging in a socially useful occupation might have provided a form of inoculation against stress. Some people who were previously of poor mental health were said to be considerably *improved* after taking up some socially necessary work: "they have a definite and satisfying job." He also adduced some evidence to show that a proportion of chronic neurotics attending outpatient clinics "had improved, since the war has given them interests previously lacking." (Rachman, pp. 24–25.)

Likewise, Eva Fogelman tells us about people who, as they were involved in rescuing Jews during World War II, seem to have found a fulfilment in their work that made them think of their own lives in more positive terms:

> For most, having saved lives was a source of quiet pride and inner satisfaction. Belgian rescuer Andrée Guelen Herscovici, who found safe hideouts for Jewish children, looks back on her rescue activity as the time in her life that stamped her character and gave her life direction. Similarly, Bert Bochove felt that rescue activities gave his life a personal fulfillment hard to duplicate: "Despite several betrayals by Dutch collaborators, in some ways the war was the best time of my life," Bochove told me. "There were always so many people around, and I got such satisfaction from helping out, from keeping the Nazis from finding the hiding place." (Fogelman, p. 274.)

We seem to find meaning in our lives by involving ourselves in projects that are important not only to us, but also to other people. And by infusing our lives with meaning, and by having ourselves guided by projects that go beyond the narrow particularities and self-centredness of our personal lives, we seem to be able to worry less about what will happen to ourselves. Hence, confronting the fear of meaninglessness should indeed be understood as a basic component of the more inclusive project of confronting the fear of personal transience. Moreover, the psychological findings cited above also seem to suggest that we should relate meaning to the pursuit of socially important projects. In this context we should also remind ourselves that certain Christian philosophers have discussed the virtue of fortitude as opposed to despair rather than to cowardice:

> The primary contrary of *fortitudo* is not cowardice but *melancholia*. Because the coward still has an energetic attachment to himself, his self-protective actions can be bold and daring. But *melancholia* and *accidie*, despair and dispiritedness, are the discouraged attitudes that the world affords nothing worth the effort of striving. (Rorty, p. 165.)

The quest for meaning involves going beyond the arbitrariness and subjectivity of the strictly personal perspective. To overcome the sense of meaninglessness, which is basically a sense of one's personal projects lacking significance, the agent must find values that can function as justified standards for her actions when considered from a wider perspective. Hence, the search for meaning is also a search for objectivity, in the sense of a search for reasons that the agent can find valid from a perspective more inclusive than her purely personal one. This search for objectively valid reasons may well take the agent beyond the values accepted in the communities with which she has so far identified, and encourage her to take a more critical view of her communal attachments. It may also motivate her to identify with more inclusive communities and conceptions of the common good (the civic community instead of the family, the community of all human agents instead of the national community, and so on).

The transcendence that takes place in this process of relating oneself to a wider perspective could be described as an internal development, in which the agent's subjective self recognizes the perspective of her objective self, and tries to accommodate its projects to the values which the objective self finds valid. This process of discovering one's objective self has been described by Thomas Nagel:

> The basic step which brings it to life is not complicated and does not require advanced scientific theories: it is simply the step of

conceiving the world as a place that includes the person I am within it, as just another of its contents – conceiving myself from outside, in other words. So I can step away from the unconsidered perspective of the particular person I thought I was.... At the first stage the intersubjectivity is still entirely human, and the objectivity is correspondingly limited. The conception is one that only other humans can share. But if the general human perspective is then placed in the same position as part of the world, the point of view from which this is done must be far more abstract, so it requires that we find within ourselves the capacity to view the world in some sense as very different creatures also might view it when abstracting from the specifics of their type of perspective. The pursuit of objectivity requires the cultivation of a rather austere universal objective self. While we can't free it entirely of infection with a particular human view and a particular historical stage, it represents a direction of possible development toward a universal conception and away from a parochial one. (Nagel, p. 63.)

While we may disagree regarding how far in the direction of full objectivity we may proceed from within our particular selves, it should not be controversial that human beings have an ability to transcend the point of view of strictly personal subjectivity. Scientific reasoning depends on such an ability, as it commits us to conclusions that will hold independently of what we personally like and dislike. But subjectivity is also transcended in moral reasoning, when we come to recognize that we have obligations emanating from the rights and interests of other people, and that we share with them a responsibility for the promotion and protection of a morally justified common good. Hence, I will suggest that the fear of meaninglessness can be confronted by an agent who is dedicated to the pursuit of a common good as conceived by the agent's objective self. Thus, when the agent is involved in projects that contribute to this common good, her actions will acquire an objective meaningfulness in the eyes of the agent herself. The contents of this objectively conceived common good remain to be specified, however. (This will be done in chapter 6.)

The Fear of Dying

Now, by being engaged in a meaningful pursuit of goals related to some conception of the common good, the agent will be able to confront one aspect of the fear of personal transience, namely, the fear that her life does not matter, that is, the fear of meaninglessness and waste. But the fear of transience, of course, also refers to the basic and natural fear of dying. This is the fear encountered on the battlefield, and to many people the paradigmatic example of courage is the soldier who unflinchingly holds his ground, although it may mean his death. In fact, in aristocratic cultures where martial bravery is held in high esteem, the virtue of courage seems to be valued because it enables the agent to die with honour, i.e., in battle, but not because it is essential in coping with more mundane threats to one's life, such as disease, old age, or accidents. It may be worth quoting Aristotle at length here, as he seems to endorse such an aristocratic conception of courage:

> What, then, are the terrors with which the courageous man is concerned? Surely the greatest, because nobody is better able to endure dreadful experiences. Now the most fearful thing of all is death; for it is the end, and it is assumed that for the dead there is no good or evil any more. But it may be thought that even death does not in all its form afford scope for courage; e.g. death at sea, or in illness. Death in what circumstances, then? Surely in the noblest; and this describes deaths in warfare, where the danger is greatest and most glorious.... So in the strict sense of the word the courageous man will be one who is fearless in the face of an honourable death, or of some sudden threat of death; and it is in war that such situations chiefly occur. Of course the courageous man will be fearless on the sea too (or in outbreaks of disease); but not in the same way as a seaman is, because the landsmen have given up all hope of being saved, and are revolted by the thought of such a death, but the seamen have high hopes because of their experience. Also courage can be shown in situations that give scope for stout resistance or a glorious death; but in a disaster of this kind [the loss of a ship] there is no place for either. (Aristotle, 1115a6–b19, pp. 127–128.)

However, we need not, and should not, adopt this narrowly aristocratic conception of courage. It is the ability to confront the fear of personal transience that should define the courage of conviction, and the focus is on the agent's experience of fear and how she copes with it, not on the nobility of the object of her fear. Hence, the fear of transience and the courage needed to confront it may be present not only in the soldier facing the enemy on the battlefield, but also in the old man alone in his home who feels his strength fade away, expecting death any day.

Of course, a person's sense of moral responsibility may well be sufficiently strong for her to face both danger and death for the sake of goals such as national independence or national survival. Think, for instance, of Patrick Pearse, sentenced to death for his part in the Irish Easter Rising of 1916, as he goes to his execution:

> Pearse stooped as he was led through the low doorway of his cell. He had already heard, with envy, one volley, telling him the first of his comrades had fallen for Ireland.
>
> Along the dark, dank corridor he went, feeling the sublimity of the moment and a love for Ireland most men reserve for wife and children, down steps that clanged like pistol shots. After that first volley, the very walls grew ears.
>
> At ground level, he was blindfolded and his hands were bound behind his back.
>
> A second volley rang out. Those around him flinched, not for him but for themselves.
>
> With a soldier on each side, he was guided briskly out into the Stonebreaker's Yard....
>
> He walked straight, with firm proud strides, without a doubt. He was doing something that would never end; he would go through death without hurt.
>
> So he smiled as he imagined Emmet had smiled. Few men lived their dream; fewer still died the death of their choice.
>
> He was halted at the north-west corner, a few feet from the wall. (de Rosa, p. 546.)

Likewise, a person of strong religious conviction may not fear confronting death and danger in violent encounters with non-believers because of her belief that she is serving God's will and the common good of all true believers.

But there is more to the fear of personal transience than just being afraid of one's death. There is the fear of the whole process which ends in one's death, that is, old age, illness, loss of mental vigour and physical strength, and so on. And if one's life has not been a meaningful one, this is likely to aggravate one's fear of dying, since death means that there will be no more chances of having a good and meaningful life. That is why the Epicureans advised people to make the most of the moment in order that they would not end up with this kind of dissatisfaction. Lucretius, for instance, connected the fear of dying to an inattentive way of life:

> But because you have always desired what you do not have, and despised what is there for the taking, your life has slipped away, incomplete and without being enjoyed, and death stands unexpectedly beside you before you can depart from your affairs replete and satisfied. (Quoted in Sharples, p. 97.)

So what about the person who has to face her death in a context that has no relation whatsoever to the furthering of any great moral goal? That is, what about the person who may well possess a sense of moral responsibility, but whose death will take place in a purely private context? This is the case of people who will face death, not on a battlefield, but in their homes, who will die not from bullets, but from old age and illness, not surrounded by brothers in arms, but alone.

Now, it is one thing to be able to mobilize one's courage when the threat to one's life can be depicted as emanating from those same evil forces which are threatening one's moral ideals. This is the battlefield courage of the soldier, fighting for what he believes to be a just cause. But deprived of this moral context and the significance it confers on one's sacrifice, or, to be more precise, deprived of the possibility of regarding one's death as a sacrifice in the first place, what solace can the agent then derive from her dedication to high ideals? In what way can her sense of moral responsibility, which motivates her to confront the fear of personal transience in the pursuit of some moral ideal, be instrumental to her as she has to confront the same fear, but without being able to connect her prospective death to this moral ideal?

It is important in this context to repeat that courage is not about being fearless, but about being able to *confront* fear. The difference between the soldier on the battlefield and the old man fading away in his home is not that the soldier does not fear his death, or that the old man fears his death more than the soldier does. It is rather a question of the extent to which the sense of moral responsibility, which helps the soldier to confront his fear of dying and to remain a self-controlling agent even in the face of death, also can be helpful to the old man whose death is not related to the pursuit of the common good.

Now, it is a very natural and basic human reaction to dislike and even to fear the prospect of one's death. Hence, to fear one's death should not by itself be taken as an indication of a lack of courage. It is only when this fear takes control of a person, filling her days with dark thoughts and her nights with sleeplessness and anxiety, locking her up in herself and depriving her of all interest in the external world, that we can speak of a loss of courage. However, although an old and diseased person, living and fading away alone, may not be able to relate to any moral purpose in the same direct way as one who is involved in, let us say, a national liberation movement, there are other ways in which her sense of moral responsibility may prove to be important.

To the extent that a person acts on her sense of moral responsibility, she is also guided by what Thomas Nagel calls the objective self. That is, her actions are guided by a belief that there are important goals of action that can be justified from a viewpoint external to her personal perspective. The agent can appreciate that she is only one agent among many, and that she has moral obligations to other agents. This is the objective self at work, telling the agent that she is neither more, nor less important than any other agent, and that her capacity for successful agency, like that of any other agent, depends on a supportive mutuality of rights and duties between agents. Moreover, as the objective self provides the agent with a sense of moral responsibility, it also provides her with the possibility of experiencing *dignity*.

As the agent decides to adhere to the moral prescriptions of the objective self, she also assumes a control of herself in accordance with the requirements of objectivity. Her actions gain in significance as they can be seen to be useful and right from an external point of view, and not only as a reflection of a purely subjective attitude. By overcoming subjectivity and acknowledging objective reasons for her actions, the agent will be able to adopt a new view of herself. She may now see herself as one who is guided by reasons that are superior to the ones generated within a purely subjective perspective. The reasons for action provided by the objective self are superior, because they are justified within an encompassing perspective which includes the agent's subjective views, but is not limited to them, as it also includes the interests of other agents. Hence, the agent who recognizes and acts in accordance with the requirements of the objective self, is able to say that her actions are guided by a conception of what is *morally right* (taking in consideration the interests of other people as well as of herself), and not just by reasons of subjective desire. (The relationship between the objective self and morality will be further discussed in chapter 5.) And it is this awareness of herself as acting for moral reasons that constitutes *the dignity of a moral agent*. By identifying with her objective self the agent accepts an obligation to have her actions guided by externally justified moral commitments. And these moral commitments may help the agent to confront the fear of personal transience, not only on the battlefield, but also in less dramatic circumstances, as it provides her with duties to fulfil that will divert her attention from her personal predicament and turn it to the good of other people.

In accordance with her dignity as a moral agent, she may, for instance, embrace the duties of democratic citizenship. These duties require, among other things, that she keeps herself informed about national as well as international affairs, and that she contributes to an enlightened discussion of these matters within her civic community, with the purpose of promoting the development of that community in accordance with the precepts of reason and justice. Hence, instead of occupying herself with self-regarding worries, the agent may affirm her moral dignity by contributing, to the best of her ability, to the common good of a democratic civic community.

Moreover, in virtue of her accepting and exercising the particular form of self-control that is involved in moral behaviour, the agent has also provided herself with another, and more general, source of dignity, namely, *the dignity of an autonomous agent*. The perception of herself as being guided by objective reasons rather than by merely subjective impulses reminds the agent of her responsibilities as an independent source of action. As Alan Gewirth has noted in a perceptive analysis of the sources of an agent's dignity:

> He pursues his ends, moreover, not as an uncontrolled reflex response to stimuli, but rather because he has chosen them after reflection on alternatives. Even if he does not always reflect, his choice can and sometimes, at least, does operate in this way. Every human agent, as such, is capable of this. Hence, the agent is an entity that, unlike other natural entities, is not, so far as he acts, subject only to external forces of nature; he can and does make his own decisions on the basis of his own reflective understanding. By virtue of these characteristics of his action, the agent has worth or dignity. (Gewirth, 1982, p. 29.)

Now, the agent's sense of her dignity as an autonomous agent may well continue to operate even in the absence of pursuits related to her moral commitments. Once she has identified with the objective self, the agent will exercise a self-control that not only prevents her self-interest from overriding her moral commitments, but, more generally, prevents her from being controlled by unreflected subjective impulses and impressions. She will find it inconsistent with her dignity as an autonomous agent to give in to moods or impulses that belittle her as a person.

Moreover, the agent's sense of moral responsibility now takes on a self-regarding dimension. The agent recognizes that she owes it to herself *qua* agent to do her best to remain an autonomous and purpose-fulfilling person:

> One should avoid regarding oneself solely as a victim, even if one's external circumstances, genetic or environmental, may warrant such a description. One should, so far as possible, try to take hold of one's own life and to guide it in the light of one's best knowledge. (Gewirth, 1998, pp. 114–115.)

Hence, the old man who is suffering from loneliness and bodily weakness, and who has little time left to live, may still refuse to complain about his lot. Instead of feeling sorry for himself, or viewing himself as a victim, he may hold on to a conception of himself as a self-controlling, responsible agent. He may continue to attend to his daily chores to the best of his abilities, endeavouring to "do something useful every day". (For this motto I am indebted to my late father, whom I thank for making me see its importance.) And by engaging himself in everyday activities, such as keeping himself and his home tidy, working in the garden, keeping up routines regarding walks, meals, and reading, and so on, the old man confirms the ideal of responsible agency, and so reinforces his dignity as an autonomous agent.

It should be noted that this is not just the courage of creativity all over again. While the agent who has the courage of creativity also tries to make the most of her powers of agency, the agent who is aware of her dignity as an autonomous agent is motivated by a perception that she *owes* it to herself to remain a self-controlling source of agency. The courage of creativity is guided by the agent's will to achieve and to make the most of her life. But it does not presuppose that the agent entertains the belief that she owes it to herself to be an achiever. The dignity of an autonomous agent, on the other hand, being derived from the courage of conviction, does not focus on agency-related achievement *per se*, but rather on preserving a certain status on the agent's part, i.e., the status of an autonomous agent. Moreover, her perception of herself as an agent with moral responsibilities regarding the recipients of her actions extends to herself, as she can conceive of her very status as an agent as an object of her own agency. Hence, the dignity of an autonomous agent involves the agent's perception of herself (or her future self) as a recipient of her actions and, consequently, as included among the objects of her moral responsibilities. Hence, she perceives herself (*qua* agent) as morally owing to herself (*qua* recipient) to respect her status as an agent and refrain from behaviour that belittles herself with respect to her capacity for the autonomous self-control that ideally characterizes an agent. This moralized self-image is absent in the courage of creativity, which takes a purely prudential view of a person's capacity for agency, encouraging her to make the most of her powers of agency, not because of any duty to herself, but simply in order to have as good a life as possible, given the aspirations, talents, and other resources that she possesses.

Accordingly, through the operations of the objective self, the agent comes to acknowledge not only the worth of certain moral commitments, but also the worth of herself, and in both cases the courage of conviction, motivated by the agent's sense of moral responsibility (for the rights of other people as well as of herself), will enable the agent to confront the fear of personal transience.

In its self-regarding version, the agent's sense of moral responsibility may induce her to develop in herself a more detached view of her personal death, consistent with the ideal of rational agency. To the extent that rational agency involves an awareness of the human condition and its inherent shortcomings, the agent's self-regarding sense of moral responsibility will motivate her to inculcate in herself a readiness to accept the fact that she will not always be able to control her destiny. With Boethius she will then recognize that

> [n]o one is so completely happy that he does not have to endure some loss. Anxiety is the necessary condition of human happiness since happiness is never completely achieved and never permanently kept. The man who enjoys great wealth may be scorned for his low birth; the man who is honored for his noble family may be oppressed by such poverty that he would rather be unknown. Someone else may enjoy both wealth and social position, but be miserable because he is not married. Still another may be happily married but have no children to inherit his fortune. Others have children, only to be saddened by their vices. Therefore, no one is entirely satisfied with his lot; each finds something lacking, or something which gives pain. (Boethius, book ii, prose 4; pp. 28–29.)

Hence, the rational agent, while doing her best to achieve her purposes, will at the same time assume a disciplined view of her human lot and not complain or pity herself regarding the various misfortunes that may befall her (although she will, of course, do what she can to overcome them). This disciplined detachment should extend also to the prospect of her own death, as dying is an inherent part of the human condition. The prospect of one's death, like other possible sources of distress, should be confronted with that stern resolution epitomized by the emperor Marcus Aurelius in his recommendation that "in every event which leads you to sorrow, remember to use this principle: that this is not a misfortune, but that to bear it like a brave man is good fortune" (*Meditations*, book iv, § 49; p. 33). In this way the agent's reactions to adversity become themselves objects of her actions, as she resolves not to give in to despair, but rather to form a dignified response to the precariousness of the human condition.

This mixture of detachment and determination, so typical of the Stoics, is magnificently demonstrated in a letter from Seneca to his friend Lucilius after the latter had fallen ill:

> It was disease of the bladder that made you apprehensive; downcast letters came from you; you were continually getting worse; I will touch the truth more closely, and say that you feared for your life. But come, did you not know, when you prayed for long life, that this was what you were praying for? A long life includes all these troubles, just as a long journey includes dust and mud and rain.... And yet life, Lucilius, is really a battle. For this reason those who are tossed about at sea, who proceed uphill and downhill over toilsome crags and heights, who go on campaigns that bring the greatest danger, are heroes and front-rank fighters; but persons who live in rotten luxury and ease while others toil, are mere turtle-doves – safe only because men despise them. (Seneca, *Ad Lucilium Epistulae Morales*, vol. III, xcvi, 3–5; p. 107.)

Now, it is important to note that Seneca's point is not to extol the experience of pain as a good in itself, but rather to advocate a certain way to confront pain when it cannot be avoided. In another letter to Lucilius he writes

> I should prefer to be free from torture; but if the time comes when it must be endured, I shall desire that I may conduct myself therein with bravery, honour, and courage. Of course I prefer that war should not occur; but if war does occur, I shall desire that I may nobly endure the wounds, the starvation, and all that the exigency of war brings. Nor am I so mad as to crave illness; but if I must suffer illness, I shall desire that I may do nothing which shows lack of restraint, and nothing that is unmanly. (Seneca, vol. II, lxvii, 4; p. 37.)

In a similar vein psychiatrist Viktor Frankl, writing against a background as a prisoner in a Nazi concentration camp, argues that

> [t]he way in which a man accepts his fate and all the suffering it entails, the way in which he takes up his cross, gives him ample opportunity – even under the most difficult circumstances – to add a deeper meaning to his life. It may remain brave, dignified and unselfish. Or in the bitter fight for self-preservation he may forget his human dignity and become no more than an animal. Here lies the chance for a man either to make use of or to forego the opportunities of attaining the moral values that a difficult situation may afford him. (Frankl, pp. 106–107.)

Now, while death, from the point of view of any agent, will remain a negative factor, as it effectively denies all prospects of future action, it is not necessarily the case that this negativity must be a source of paralysing fear and terror for agents. The agent who assumes responsibility for herself, including her attitudes towards life and death, will carefully examine these attitudes, subjecting them to criticism in accordance with the canons of inductive and deductive reasoning. Among other things, the agent will ask herself *why*, exactly, death is supposed to be fearful. Death, being the negation of life and all the sensations of life, cannot by itself constitute a negative sensation: the negation of sensation is no sensation, not a particular kind of negative sensation. According to this line of reasoning, fearing death is worse than death itself, since fearing death implies the presence of a negative sensation, while death itself implies the absence of all kinds of sensation. Hence, Epicurus seems to be on the right track, when he points to the irrationality of the common attitude towards death:

> Become accustomed to the belief that death is nothing to us. For all good and evil consists in sensation, but death is deprivation of sensation. And therefore a right understanding that death is nothing to us makes the mortality of life enjoyable, not because it adds to it an infinite span of time, but because it takes away the craving for immortality. For there is nothing terrible in life for the man who has truly comprehended that there is nothing terrible in not living. So that the man speaks but idly who says that he fears death not because it will be painful when it comes, but because it is painful in anticipation. For that which gives no trouble when it comes, is but an empty pain in anticipation. So death, the most terrifying of ills, is nothing to us, since so long as we exist, death is not with us; but when death comes, then we do not exist. It does not then concern either the living or the dead, since for the former it is not, and the latter are no more. (Bailey, p. 85; Bailey's translation is from Diogenes Laertius, *Lives of Eminent Philosophers*, vol. II, book x, §§ 124–125; p. 651.)

Now, it could be objected that all that Epicurus has shown is that the *state of being dead* is nothing to fear. But it remains to be shown that we have no reason to fear the *process of dying*, which indeed may be painful. (Think, for instance, of someone who is tortured to death on the rack.) Of course, Epicurus addresses the problem of pain, but in a rather dismissive way:

> Pain does not last continuously in the flesh, but the acutest pain is there for a very short time, and even that which just exceeds the pleasure in the flesh does not continue for many days at once. (Bailey, p. 95; Diogenes Laertius, book x, § 140; p. 665.)

Perhaps all that Epicurus means is that if the pain is sufficiently bad, we will simply pass out and so be free from suffering. Severe pain could also be an indication of imminent death, and then the result will be the same: the pain will not last for long. Still, people are likely to differ in their views of what constitutes "extreme pain", just as they are likely to differ regarding how much comfort can be derived from Epicurus' assertion that extreme pain will last only "a very short time". A month of severe pain may be endurable to some people, but not to others. What if a person will be in a debilitating state of pain for months, or even years, before she finally dies? Is she still supposed to take comfort in Epicurean wisdom?

Now, Epicurus may seem less than satisfactory in his way of dealing with the problem of suffering. On the other hand, we should ask ourselves if we are pursuing the right problem here. If we aspire to a form of courage that enables us to confront our fear of personal transience, we should learn how to dispense with guarantees rather than looking for certainty in these matters. We should not ask: "How can I be sure that I will never suffer from debilitating pain?", since this very question gives away a lack of the relevant form of courage. It is fear of pain that prompts us to ask for guarantees against pain. Moreover, once the question is asked, we immediately realize (if we are rational) that nobody can provide the guarantee required. We cannot make ourselves immune to the possibility of pain, not even pain of the most extreme kind. Hence, for reasons of rationality alone, we should refrain from asking for something that cannot possibly be given to us.

Moreover, reminding ourselves of the principle of constructive creativity and its insistence on making the most of things, given the opportunities at hand, we should focus on what to do here and now, rather than worrying about the possibility of disaster in the near or distant future. Hence, we should heed Aristotle's advice, that

> the truly good and wise man bears all his fortunes with dignity, and always takes the most honourable course that circumstances permit; just as a good general uses his available forces in the most militarily effective way, and a good shoemaker makes the neatest

shoe out of the leather supplied to him, and the same with all the other kinds of craftsmen. (Aristotle, 1100b27–1101a20, p. 84.)

And, as Epicurus would tell us, we only add to our pains if we worry about possible future pain. For the same reason Seneca admonishes his friend Lucilius "not to be unhappy before the crisis comes" (vol. I, xiii, 4–5; p. 75). We cannot provide ourselves with guarantees that we will never suffer pain, but we can at least try to rid ourselves of the specific pain of *worrying* about future pain. To this end, we should develop in ourselves the attitudes of positive actualism and positive possibilism, mentioned earlier as components of the courage of creativity. These attitudes can, by reminding us that our lot is not the worst possible and that good outcomes indeed are possible, function as a valuable antidote to worries about future disasters.

Returning to the importance of being able to sense one's dignity as an autonomous agent, we should note that this argument is rather similar to the views defended by Ralph Waldo Emerson in his essay on self-reliance. Emerson, for instance, writes that

> There is a time in every man's education when he arrives at the conviction that envy is ignorance; that imitation is suicide; that he must take himself for better, for worse, as his portion; that though the wide universe is full of good, no kernel of nourishing corn can come to him but through his toil bestowed on that plot of ground which is given to him to till. The power which resides in him is new in nature, and none but he knows what that is which he can do, nor does he know until he has tried. (Emerson, pp. 27–28.)

Emerson stresses the importance of the agent developing a proper sense of responsibility regarding the contents of her own life. And interestingly enough, he implicitly analyses self-reliance as a form of courage in his rejection of those who are satisfied to rely on beliefs received from others, i.e., those who do not rely on themselves: "God will not have his work made manifest by cowards" (p. 28).

However, we should note that when Emerson goes on to discuss heroism, he adopts an élitist and martial view of courage that differs in important respects from the one we are outlining here. Heroism, in the form that Emerson advocates, comes close to the Aristotelian view of courage:

> Its rudest form is the contempt for safety and ease, which makes the attractiveness of war. It is a self-trust which slights the restraints of prudence in the plenitude of its energy and power to repair the harms it may suffer.... Heroism feels and never reasons, and therefore is always right; and although a different breeding, different religion, and greater intellectual activity, would have modified, or even reversed the particular action, yet for the hero, that thing he does, is the highest deed, and is not open to the censure of philosophers or divines. (Emerson, p. 148.)

The courage of conviction, as it has been analysed above, does not imply this Emersonian anti-rationalism. On the contrary, as it emanates from the objective self, it requires that the agent should be able to confront the fear of personal transience only for moral reasons that can be identified and justified from a perspective that is external to the agent's subjective point of view. Hence, it should not be governed simply by what the agent "feels", but rather by the agent's critical assessment of what is sufficiently valuable to be worth sacrificing oneself for. Courage should not be reduced to the unreflective self-assertion of the individual hero, which Emerson seems to have in mind.

Consequently, the courage of conviction does not require of the agent that she should act in accordance with the "high counsel" related by Emerson: "Always do what you are afraid to do" (p. 154). The courage of conviction is not about proving something to oneself or to others. It is not about showing off bravado. Instead it is about acknowledging responsibility for oneself, for other people, and for the community or communities of which one is a member, and which deserve one's allegiance. This requires careful deliberation and reasoned argument on the agent's part, in contrast to the heroic emotional self-righteousness advocated by Emerson.

It is noteworthy, however, that Emerson has not been without modern followers. One who seems to have appreciated his views on courage was Robert Kennedy. Not only did he underline the passage about always doing what you are afraid to do in his copy of Emerson's *Essays*, but he "made a cult of courage" in his personal life. Kennedy's cult of courage did not limit itself to an unwillingness to protect himself against assassins, but also included climbing the 13,900 feet high Mount Kennedy, in spite of being "deathly afraid of heights" (Thomas, pp. 18–19; 306–308).

The Fear of Social Death

The preceding section has dealt with the courage of conviction as it relates to the agent's ability to confront her fear of personal transience when this fear is interpreted as the fear of dying in the physical sense, i.e., of ceasing to live in the most basic and biological sense. However, we should be aware that the concept of personal transience has a wider application than physical death. Just as we may talk of a person's *social life*, that may provide her with love, affection, friendship, and other important aspects of a good life, so we may talk of a person's *social death*, when all these goods are removed from her as other people turn their backs on her and refuse to have anything to do with her. And to many people the threat of ostracism and social disapproval may appear almost as fearsome as a threat to their physical lives. Hence, the fear of social disapproval may also function as a powerful check on an agent's willingness to follow her conscience when doing so is likely to leave her an outcast of society. Accordingly, we may speak of an agent's possession of the courage of conviction not only when her sense of moral responsibility motivates her to confront her fear of dying in the physical sense, but also when it motivates her to confront her fear of social death. This is what Henry Sidgwick seems to have in mind, when he refers to "the 'moral courage' by which men face the pains and dangers of social disapproval in the performance of what they believe to be duty" (Sidgwick, p. 333, n. 3.)

John F. Kennedy's book *Profiles in Courage* presents a series of cases representative of this aspect of the courage of conviction, gathered from the political lives of American senators from John Quincey Adams to Robert A. Taft. These senators, for all their other differences, shared a common trait of character, namely, an unwillingness to compromise their conceptions of duty and right for the sake of popularity or party loyalty.

One of these courageous senators was Edmund G. Ross, who defied his fellow Republican senators as well as his Kansas constituency by voting "Not guilty" in the impeachment process against President Andrew Johnson in 1868, thereby thwarting the attempt to depose the president. Andrew Johnson had made himself unpopular with Congress as he tried to prevent the so-called Radical Republicans from imposing too harsh conditions of reconstruction on the defeated Southern States. The conflict between the president and Congress came to a climax in the autumn of 1867, as Johnson asked for the resignation of the secretary of war, Edwin M. Stanton, whom he suspected of being a tool of the Radical Republicans. Stanton refused to resign, and sought support in Congress. Now Congress had some months before enacted (over the president's veto) the Tenure-of-Office Bill, according to which the president could not, without the consent of the senate, remove from office any office-holder whose appointment required confirmation by the senate. Now, although cabinet members were exempted from this bill, the dismissal of Stanton was invoked by the president's enemies in Congress as a justifying ground for impeaching him for having violated the Tenure-of-Office Bill. As the impeachment process began in the spring of 1868, each senator had to take an oath "to do impartial justice". However, "as the trial progressed, it became increasingly apparent that the impatient Republicans did not intend to give the president a fair trial on the formal issues upon which the impeachment was drawn, but intended instead to depose him from the White House on any grounds, real or imagined, for refusing to accept their policies" (Kennedy, pp. 132–133). A two-thirds majority in the senate was required for a conviction. As the senate was composed at that time, a two-thirds majority meant 36 votes. And this was exactly the number the Radical Republicans expected to be able to muster. They never expected any trouble from Edmund G. Ross. An early anti-slavery activist, a Union volunteer in the Civil War (from which he emerged a major), a consistent adherent of the Radical Republicans in the senate (he had voted for all their measures), a representative of the anti-Johnson state of Kansas, and himself highly critical of the president, there should have been no doubt regarding Ross's position. However, Ross also took his oath about doing impartial justice seriously. As he remarked to a senatorial colleague at the beginning of the impeachment process:

> Well, Sprague, the thing is here; and, so far as I am concerned, though a Republican and opposed to Mr. Johnson and his policy, he shall have as fair a trial as an accused man ever had on this earth. (Quoted in Kennedy, p. 134.)

As the Radical Republicans could not afford to lose a single senator, Ross's declared intention to keep an open mind regarding the president's guilt worried them as well as the anti-Johnson camp in general. Ross soon found himself under pressure from colleagues, newpapers, and his own Kansas constituency, as the day (16 May 1868) approached when the senate was to vote on the president being guilty or not guilty of the charges brought against him.

> The night before the Senate was to take its first vote for the conviction or acquittal of Johnson, Ross received this telegram from home:
>
>> Kansas has heard the evidence and demands the conviction of the President.
>> (*signed*) D. R. ANTHONY AND 1,000 OTHERS
>
> And on that fateful morning of May 16 Ross replied:
>
>> To D. R. Anthony and 1,000 Others: I do not recognize your right to demand that I vote either for or against conviction. I have taken an oath to do impartial justice according to the Constitution and laws, and trust that I shall have the courage to vote according to the dictates of my judgment and for the highest good of the country.
>> [signed] – E. G. Ross
>
> That morning spies traced Ross to his breakfast; and ten minutes before the vote was taken his Kansas colleague warned him in the

presence of Thaddeus Stevens [a prominent Radical Republican] that a vote for acquittal would mean trumped up charges and his political death. (Kennedy, pp. 136–137.)

However, Ross voted "Not guilty", and Andrew Johnson was thereby acquitted and allowed to sit his term out. Edmund Ross was subsequently the victim of much abuse. His motives were questioned. He was accused of corruption and treason. A Justice of the Kansas Supreme Court suggested in a telegram to Ross that he ought to kill himself. He was vilified in the press as a "miserable poltroon and traitor" (p. 141). And when he returned to Kansas in 1871, as Kennedy notes, "he and his family suffered social ostracism, physical attack, and near poverty" (p. 142). So, why did Ross vote "Not guilty" on that May 16 1868? Years later he developed his reasons. They centre upon the importance of having an independent executive office that is not a mere tool for rival factions within Congress, and that can remain a bulwark against such factions:

> If ... the President must step down ... a disgraced man and a political outcast ... upon insufficient proofs and from partisan considerations, the office of President would be degraded, cease to be a coordinate branch of the government, and ever after subordinated to the legislative will. It would practically have revolutionized our splendid political fabric into a partisan Congressional autocracy. (Quoted in Kennedy, p. 141.)

Edmund Ross acted out of a sense of moral responsibility. He confronted a particular version of the fear of personal transience which concerns ceasing to be, not in a physical sense but in a social sense. More specifically, he confronted the fear of political ostracism and public dishonour. He was warned that voting for acquittal meant "political death", and yet he would not compromise. In his unwillingness to go against his conscience and his political ideals, he manifested a courage of conviction.

Interestingly enough, the man whom Edmund Ross saved, President Andrew Johnson, could also serve as an example of this version of the courage of conviction. He had once, as a senator of Tennessee, been one of very few prominent Southern politicians to defend the Union even as his own home state prepared for secession:

> As the Union began to crack in 1860 ... Andrew Johnson, alone among the Southerns, spoke for Union. When his train, as he returned home to Tennessee to fight to keep his state in the Union, stopped at Lynchburg, Virginia, an angry mob dragged the Senator from his car, assaulted and abused him, and decided not to lynch him only at the last minute, with the rope already around his neck, when they agreed that hanging him was the privilege of his own neighbors in Tennessee. Throughout Tennessee, Johnson was hissed, hooted, and hanged in effigy. Confederate leaders were assured that "His power is gone and henceforth there will be nothing left but the stench of the traitor." Oblivious to the threat of death, Andrew Johnson toured the state, attempting in vain to stem the tide against secession, and finally becoming the only Southern Senator who refused to secede with his state. On his return trip to Washington, greeted by an enthusiastic crowd at the station in Cincinnati, he told them proudly: "I am a citizen of the South and of the state of Tennessee.... [But] I am also a citizen of the United States." (Kennedy, pp. 227–228.)

In Andrew Johnson's case, he had to confront the fear of personal transience in both the physical and the social sense, and his sense of moral responsibility for the preservation of the Union seems to have enabled him to do so. There are certain similarities between Johnson's uncompromising sense of moral responsibility, and that of the villagers of Le Chambon, who refused to hand over Jewish refugees to the Nazis during the German occupation:

> The two buses parked in the wide village square, and the police captain called on the head minister of the village and demanded that he give him a list of all the Jews in the village. The Huguenot pastor refused. Then the police captain ordered the minister to sign an official poster that told all the Jews in the village to turn themselves in to the police in order to avoid risking the lives of the families who had been sheltering them.... Again the minister

refused. The police chief warned the pastor that if he did not sign the poster within twenty-four hours, he and his fellow minister would be arrested – by noon of the next day, Sunday.

The police slept in their buses all Saturday night, and on Sunday morning they raided the houses of the village looking for Jews. But during the night the Jews had been evacuated into the woods around Le Chambon, and the police could find only one Jew to put in their big buses. While he sat in the bus the villagers shoved gifts – mainly food – through the window by his seat. Soon there was a heap of gifts beside him. Later the buses left, with the one prisoner and his precious gifts. (Hallie, pp. 24–25.)

To sum up, the courage of conviction is the courage of men and women who die for their nations or for their religious beliefs, who go to jail rather than making a deal with injustice, who sacrifice popularity to principles, and who prefer a life in poverty to one sullied by corruption. The courage of conviction is also the courage of men and women who stand up and assist those who are subjected to maltreatment at the hands of robbers or street thugs, even at the risk of drawing negative attention to themselves and suffering bodily harm in the process.

On the other hand, and this is important to note, it is also the courage of the fanatic, who regardless of the cost to himself or to others, carries out his plans, which may well include the killing of hundreds or even thousands of innocent people. Hence, the courage of conviction may well be put to immoral use, a complication to which we will return later in this book.

In comparison to the courage of creativity, we should also note that the courage of conviction does not imply that the agent necessarily acts in a spirit of agency-related optimism. The courage of conviction is guided by a sense of moral responsibility rather than by a sense of positive possibilism (although, as we noted above, positive attitudes are indeed a great help in our efforts to confront the fear of personal transience). The strength of the agent's sense of moral responsibility, combined with her assumptions of what morality requires of her in the situation at hand, makes it psychologically *necessary* for her to act as she does, whether or not she is able to picture a successful outcome of her actions. Of course, it is possible that one and the same agent possesses both the courage of creativity and the courage of conviction, and that, consequently, she is driven both by an optimistic will to achieve and a sense of moral responsibility. But it could also be the case that the person who possesses one of the two forms of courage lacks the other, and hence that the will to achieve appears without a sense of moral responsibility and vice versa. Thus, the person whose agency-related optimism has assisted her in making a splendid career in business may lack the sense of moral responsibility necessary to join the army when her country is being attacked. And the timid person who never got her career under way due to her lack of optimism, may turn out to be a fanatic in religious matters, ready to die for her religious convictions about man's duty to obey God's will.

We will return to the relationship between the two forms of courage later on. First, however, we must clarify how the objective self may be of help in the process of moral reasoning and justification. To risk one's own life and the lives of others in the service of some common good is commendable only to the extent that the common good in question deserves our allegiance. Now, the common good of, for instance, a Nazi community differs from the common good of a liberal democratic community, and the arguments invoked to justify allegiance to the one type of community are likely to contradict the arguments invoked in support of the other. Hence, our discussion of the value of courage cannot be complete without a discussion of the requirements of morality.

CHAPTER 5

The Objective Self and Moral Reasoning

In the preceding chapter, the concept of the objective self played an important role in my discussion of the courage of conviction. The objective self, by making the agent aware of her obligations to other people, and by motivating her to fulfil these obligations, helps her confront the various dimensions of the fear of personal transience. Still, it could be objected that my argument so far is inconclusive. Granted, the agent may detach from her strictly personal point of view and perceive herself as just one agent among many others, neither more, nor less important than anybody else. But why should this detachment be expected to generate a conception of moral obligations? After all, the agent's detachment from her personal perspective might simply leave her with a bewildering experience of being just a grain of sand in the desert, without any sense of a shared mutuality of rights and duties.

Moreover, there is the problem of the process of detachment itself. If it is too limited, agents are likely to be influenced by their being situated in a particular social and cultural environment at a particular time, and hence their objective selves will not be sufficiently objective to free them of the prejudices of their time and place. On the other hand, if the process is taken too far, it may result in a purely physical perspective of the world, according to which matter and atomic structures may be granted an objective existence, but certainly not moral values, as they will be seen to depend on a human perspective and any human perspective, no matter if it is universally adopted by all humans, will necessarily look limited and subjective when compared to the purely physical perspective. In the first case, we cannot trust the values accepted by the objective self to be truly objectively justified. In the second case, we will get no values at all from the objective self. Hence, we must find an appropriate process of detachment that is capable of fulfilling the requirements of objectivity to a satisfying extent without leaving the perspective of human agency behind altogether.

Now, the aspiration for an objective understanding of the world and the efforts to ground morality on a set of values or principles that can be given an objective justification are, I believe, deeply related to the combination of man's awareness of his fallibility and his quest for certainty. As we come to recognize the distinction between what we *think* is true and right and what *is* true and right (for instance, in cases where, in the light of new facts or a new understanding of the facts, we find reason to correct an earlier judgement), we are motivated to look for a reliable method of reasoning which will help us to critically assess the contents of our impressions of the world and our intuitions about what we ought to do. As we try to detach ourselves from our immediate views in order to form a critically informed opinion, we automatically move in the direction of objectivity. As Thomas Nagel points out,

> Objectivity is a method of understanding. It is beliefs and attitudes that are objective in the primary sense. Only derivatively do we call objective the truths that can be arrived at in this way. To acquire a more objective understanding of some aspect of life or the world, we step back from our initial view of it and form a new conception which has that view and its relation to the world as its object. In other words, we place ourselves in the world that is to be understood. The old view then comes to be regarded as an appearance, more subjective than the new view, and correctable or confirmable by reference to it. The process can be repeated, yielding a still more objective conception. (Nagel, p. 4.)

Objectivity is about detaching oneself from one's purely personal point of view, and adopting a way of thinking and reasoning which includes that point of view as one among many others. In this sense, morality represents an increase in objectivity, to the extent that moral reasoning is about finding out what is impersonally right and wrong, impartially adjudicating the conflicting right-claims or interests of different persons.

When we engage in a detached reasoning of this kind, our objective selves are at work. Now, we are, I believe, more familiar with the *activities* of the objective self, than we are with the *term* "objective self". Whenever we step outside of the immediately given, and try to think critically about our desires (instead of just acting on them), the objective self comes into play. Prudential reasoning, as when we decide to suppress some present desire for the sake of a future and more important goal, is an example of the functioning of the objective self. And, as Nagel notes, to the extent that prudential reasoning helps us secure control over our actions, the objective self is also a source of freedom:

> The conflict between prudence and impulse is not like the conflict between chicken salad and salami, for it is a conflict between levels: the immediate perspective of the present moment and the (partly) transcendent perspective of temporal neutrality among the foreseeable moments of one's life. It is an example of the pursuit of freedom because through prudence we try to stand back from the impulses that press on us immediately, and to act in a temporal sense from outside of ourselves. If we could not do this, we would as agents be trapped in the present moment, with temporal neutrality reduced to a vantage point of observation. (Nagel, pp. 132–133.)

However, since the objective self is a part of us, and since we are finite beings with inherent limits to our capacity for self-transcendence, there are also limits to the objective self and its powers. There are some aspects of life that cannot be grasped from a completely detached perspective, but can only be comprehended by the subjective self. It is one thing to conclude from a person's outward appearance that she is depressed, but it is an altogether different thing to pronounce on what it is like *for her* to be depressed. As Nagel comments,

> If we try to understand experience from an objective viewpoint that is distinct from that of the subject of the experience, then even if

we continue to credit its perspectival nature, we will not be able to grasp its most specific qualities unless we can imagine them subjectively. We will not know exactly how scrambled eggs taste to a cockroach even if we develop a detailed objective phenomenology of the cockroach sense of taste. (Nagel, p. 25.)

Now these limits of the objective self might appear as a serious obstacle if we want to discuss the validity of moral values (for instance, the common good) in terms of what can be endorsed by the objective self. That is, it would so appear if we took it for granted that moral values were like sensations of taste, and could only be understood from a subjectively emotive point of view. However, this is not Nagel's view. On the contrary, since moral values are related to important human interests, they can be perceived as values also when the agent detaches from the particularity of her personal viewpoint. Hence, moral values can be grasped by the objective self.

> Values express the objective will. Ethical values in particular result from the combination of many lives and sets of interests in a single set of judgments. The demands of balancing, coordination, and integration that this imposes have consequences for what can be objectively willed for each individual, and therefore for oneself. Ethics is one route to objective engagement because it supplies an alternative to pure observation of ourselves from outside. It permits the will to expand at least some of the way along the path of transcendence possible for the understanding. (Nagel, p. 136.)

Of course, there are many values that can be understood only from a personal and subjective perspective. To want to be the first man on the planet Mars, or the most famous philosopher ever, are goals that are very unlikely candidates for objective affirmation. It is possible to observe, from the detached point of view of the objective self, that there are people who actually have preferences like these. But it is one thing to confirm that someone has a particular preference, and it is another thing to identify with that preference from an external point of view. And the contents of the preferences given above are too specific, too tied up to a personal perspective, to be affirmed from the detached perspective inhabited by the objective self. However, there are reasons for action that can be understood and affirmed by the objective self. These are, in Nagel's terminology, *agent-neutral* reasons, as they do not include "an essential reference" to the person having them (Nagel, p. 152). Examples of agent-neutral reasons are, according to Nagel, the pursuit of pleasure and the avoidance of pain. These kinds of reason are sufficiently basic to be endorsed from an external viewpoint, i.e., by the objective self:

> [T]he pain, though it comes attached to a person and his individual perspective, is just as clearly hateful to the objective self as to the subjective individual. I know what it's like even when I contemplate myself from outside, as one person among countless others. And the same applies when I think about anyone else in this way. The pain can be detached in thought from the fact that it is mine without losing any of its dreadfulness. (Nagel, p. 160.)

Nagel's point is that aiming for pleasure and shunning pain will be accepted as reasons for action even from a viewpoint which is detached from all subjectivity. These reasons do not presuppose any particular, personal set of preferences and aversions to be accepted as valid. Hence, they can be not only understood but accepted and affirmed by the objective self:

> When the objective self contemplates pain, it has to do so through the perception of the sufferer, and the sufferer's reaction is very clear. Of course he wants to be rid of *this pain* unreflectively – not because he thinks it would be good to reduce the amount of pain in the world. But at the same time his awareness of how bad it is doesn't essentially involve the thought of it as his. The desire to be rid of pain has only the pain as its object. This is shown by the fact that it doesn't even require the idea of *oneself* in order to make sense: if I lacked or lost the conception of myself as distinct from other possible or actual persons, I could still apprehend the badness of pain, immediately. So when I consider it from an objective standpoint, the ego doesn't get between the pain and the objective

self. My objective attitude toward pain is rightly taken over from the immediate attitude of the subject, and naturally takes the form of an evaluation of the pain itself, rather than merely a judgment of what would be reasonable for its victim to want: "*This experience ought not to go on, whoever is having it.*" (Nagel, p. 161.)

In addition to pleasure and pain, there are some other basic factors of human welfare, such as freedom and access to opportunities necessary to a fulfilling life, which, according to Nagel, will generate agent-neutral reasons:

> From the objective standpoint, the fundamental thing leading to the recognition of agent-neutral reasons is a sense that no one is more important than anyone else. The question then is whether we are all equally unimportant or all equally important, and the answer, I think, is somewhere in between. The areas in which we must continue to be concerned about ourselves and others from outside are those whose value comes as close as possible to being universal. If impersonal value is going to be admitted at all, it will naturally attach to liberty, general opportunities, and the basic resources of life, as well as to pleasure and the absence of suffering. This is not equivalent to assigning impersonal value to each person's getting whatever he wants. (Nagel, pp. 171–172.)

However, there is one part of common-sense morality which Nagel's version of the objective self seems unable to fully incorporate, namely, deontology, that is, our obligations to respect the rights of other people not to be killed, injured, imprisoned, threatened, tortured, coerced, lied to, etc. Given his distinction between agent-neutral reasons (deriving from objectively valid interests) and agent-relative reasons (deriving from the personal projects and preferences of a particular agent), Nagel finds deontological constraints "formally puzzling":

> We can understand how autonomous agent-relative reasons might derive from the specific projects and concerns of the agent, and we can understand how neutral reasons might derive from the interests

of others, giving each of us reason to take them into account. But how can there be relative reasons to respect the claims of others? How can there be a reason not to twist someone's arm which is not equally a reason to prevent his arm from being twisted by someone else? (Nagel, p. 178.)

Nagel's problem is that deontological constraints are addressed to the agent, giving *her* a reason not to do something: "You should not twist his arm". Hence, the reason given is agent-relative. Deontology, according to Nagel, does not presume that there is a universal value in preventing arms from being twisted. Accordingly, deontology does not presume that we all have a reason to see to it that a particular person's arm is not twisted. It is only to the agent who is about to twist someone's arm that the deontological prescription is directed: "*You* have a reason not to twist his arm":

> It is hard to understand how there could be such a thing. One would expect that reasons stemming from the interests of others would be neutral and not relative. How can a claim based on the interests of others apply to those who may infringe it directly or intentionally in a way that it does not apply to those whose actions may damage that same interest just as much indirectly? After all, it is no worse *for the victim* to be killed or injured deliberately than accidentally, or as an unavoidable sideeffect of the dangerous rescue operation. (Nagel, p. 178.)

However, there is more to Nagel's criticism than just a complaint about deontology upsetting his classification of various types of reasons. The more substantial part of his criticism is that subjectivity is allowed to block the workings of the objective self by means of deontological constraints. That is, although I may be able to bring about an objectively better outcome, such as (in Nagel's example) saving the lives of some friends by twisting a child's arm, deontology holds that I am doing something morally wrong in twisting the child's arm. The deontological view of what *I* have a reason to do hence gets in the way of the impersonal way of reasoning that looks only at the overall result, regardless of whether that result is brought about by me or by someone or something else.

> The issue is whether the special, personal perspective of agency has legitimate significance in determining what people have reason to do – whether, because of this perspective, I can have sufficient reason not to do something which, considered from an external standpoint, it would be better if I did. That is, *things* will be better, what *happens* will be better, if I twist the child's arm than if I do not. But I will have done something worse.... The paradox is that this partial, perspectival respect for the interests of others should not give way to an agent-neutral respect free of perspective. The deontological perspective seems primitive, even superstitious, by comparison: merely a stage on the way to full objectivity. How can what we *do* in this narrow sense be so important? (Nagel, pp. 180–181.)

But we must probe deeper here. Is it really impossible for the objective self to incorporate deontological considerations? If I detach myself from my personal perspective with its idiosyncracies and subjective preferences and aversions, I am still able to conceive of the world as containing more than just outcomes and consequences. I am able to conceive of the world as an arena of agency and agents. And even if I (or, rather, my objective self) cannot identify with all the individual purposes of particular agents, I am able to form a view of certain general features of agency, including the generally necessary conditions of successful action, which hence will be relevant to all agents. Accordingly, the objective self will be capable of perceiving an evaluative perspective common to all agents, regardless of their varying particular purposes. From this evaluative perspective the necessary conditions of successful action will be conceived of as *necessary goods*, i.e., as objects that are not only indispensable but also valuable. Since the agent must consider the realization of her particular goal of action as a good (she acts, i.e., engages in behaviour that is both voluntary and purposive, because she *wants* to achieve her goal, that is, she regards the realization of her goal as something good in the sense that its realization is preferred to its non-realization), the conditions that are generally necessary for all successful action must be regarded as necessary goods, and they must be so regarded by all agents. Hence, no agent can, *qua* agent, accept that she is deprived of these necessary goods. In the words of Alan Gewirth:

> Where the particular purposes for which different persons act may vary widely, the capabilities of action required for fulfilling their purposes and for maintaining and increasing their abilities are the same for all persons.... The need for and positive evaluation of these capabilities are hence common to all such agents amid their diversities of particular purposes and values.... To this extent, the relativity objection fails: goods viewed generically-dispositionally as the general capabilities of action are necessarily and objectively goods for all purposive agents. (Gewirth, 1978, p. 59.)

According to Gewirth's analysis, *freedom* (the ability to control one's behaviour by one's unforced choice) and *well-being* (including not only life, physical integrity, and mental equilibrium, but also the ability to maintain undiminished one's capabilities for action, e.g., not being cheated or stolen from, as well as the ability to increase one's capabilities for action, e.g., by enjoying self-esteem and having access to education and being able to provide for oneself) constitute the generic features and necessary conditions of successful action "when such action is regularly and predictably accomplished" (1978, p. 62). Hence, all rational agents must (logically), given their necessary positive evaluation of their particular goals of action, regard freedom and well-being as necessary goods.

Now, at the level of particular actions agents differ regarding what goals they want to achieve and, accordingly, they differ in their views of particular goods. While some agents want to climb mountains, others are content to collect stamps. But common to all agents is their need for the conditions generally necessary for successful action, as they want to succeed in their various purposes. Hence, all agents must regard freedom and well-being as necessary goods. Moreover, as freedom and well-being are *necessary* goods, no agent can (logically) accept that she is deprived of them. Hence, all agents must, *qua* agents, claim rights to freedom and well-being. And since the sufficient condition for the agent's rights-claim is that she is an agent with purposes that she wants to fulfil, she must (logically) accept the universalized claim: "All agents have rights to freedom and well-being". These rights, being derived from the generic features of successful agency, are the *generic rights* which all agents are logically required to accept and respect. Hence, all agents must accept as a binding moral prescription the *Principle of Generic Consistency (PGC)*, which states: "Act in accord with the generic rights of your recipients as well as of yourself" (Gewirth, 1978, p. 135; for a detailed account of Gewirth's argument, see Gewirth, 1978, pp. 48–128, as well as the careful reconstruction of the argument in Beyleveld, 1991).

The agent who accepts the *PGC* has thereby also accepted a prescription emanating from the objective self, as she has detached herself from the confines of her personal purposes and, by means of logical reason, arrived at a normative conclusion valid for all agents. The universalization involved in moving from an evaluation of one's personal and immediate goals of action to accepting the rights of all agents to freedom and well-being, is indeed a tribute to man's capacity for objectivity and to the powers of that capacity. Given this view of the objective self as an *objective agent-self*, we are able to solve Nagel's problem with deontology. Deontological constraints derived from the *PGC*, such as prohibitions regarding killing, injuring, and stealing, are indeed agent-neutral, in the sense that they hold for all agents, and their validity can be ascertained by any agent applying her powers of logical reasoning to the concept of agency. Hence, returning to Nagel's example of a person who considers the possibility of twisting a child's arm in order to save the lives of his friends, the objective agent-self would uphold the deontological constraint that it is wrong to twist the child's arm, since doing so would constitute a violation of the child's rights to freedom and well-being.

Nagel seems to think that whenever we opt for an alternative that is less than optimal on purely consequentialist terms (letting several people die rather than twisting a child's arm), we could not be guided by the objective self. But the objective self need not be construed as a maximizer of good consequences with no regard for how these consequences are distributed. Instead it could be construed as an objective agent-self, which, although it is detached from the particular purposes of individual agents, remains within the general sphere of agency and is capable of adopting a normative perspective that necessarily holds for all agents, assigning to them mutual rights and duties.

The objective agent-self rejects outcomes which involve the violation of important rights of innocent agents, and it does so from the objective viewpoint of rational agency. Hence, the child's arm should not be twisted since doing so would violate the child's physical integrity, and hence her right to basic well-being. This does not mean that nothing should be done to save the lives of the other persons in Nagel's example. But it does mean that their lives must not be saved at the cost of having an innocent child's basic rights violated. (In Nagel's example the child is in no way responsible for the fate of the other people. They are badly hurt in a car accident, and the twisting of the child's arm is thought of as a means to coerce the child's grandmother to hand over the keys to her car, with which the injured persons can be brought to a hospital and so have their lives saved. The grandmother's reluctance to hand over the keys is explained by her being terrified by the desperation of the person who wants to save his friends. As a consequence, she has locked herself in the bathroom, leaving the child at the mercy of the desperate stranger.)

From the point of view of the objective agent-self we may indeed be permitted to steal a car if that would be necessary to save the lives of our friends, since life is more important to the possibility of successful action than to have all of one's property left intact. The objective agent-self will handle conflicts of rights by assessing the relative needfulness for action of the goods protected by the rights in question. Consequently, the right to life takes precedence over the right to property in cases of conflict. (However, it should be noted that it is only when it is *necessary*, and only to the *extent* that is necessary, to the preservation of the more important right that the less important right should be overridden.) But when we are confronted with a choice either to twist a child's arm or to let our friends die, the conflict at hand is one between rights at the same level of basic importance for action, involving the physical integrity of both parties to the conflict. And we are not permitted to remedy one case of violated physical integrity by ourselves violating the physical integrity of a third person, that is, unless the third person is an aggressor against whom we are entitled to defend ourselves. (In that case, the aggressor has, by his own transgression of the *PGC*, forfeited his right not to be interfered with.) Hence, we are not permitted to twist the child's arm. (For Gewirth's discussion of various criteria for solving conflicts of duties, see Gewirth, 1978, pp. 342–354.)

Now, it could be objected that the conflict in Nagel's example is not about goods at the same level of importance. After all, the persons injured in the accident will die unless they are brought to hospital, while the discomfort that we cause the child by twisting her arm is limited both as regards its duration (assuming that the child's grandmother will give in when she hears the child screaming) and as regards its long-term effects (a bruised arm which will heal in a day or two).

As an answer to this objection, it should be pointed out that as long as we are twisting the child's arm, and as long as the grandmother's behaviour is controlled by what we do to her grandchild, we are thereby also depriving them of their status as agents. Being denied the possibility of engaging themselves in action, i.e., voluntary and purposive behaviour, their means of response are limited to *reactions*, such as screams, anxiety, rage, and other forms of panic-guided emotions. We are indeed inflicting harm of the most basic kind on the child and her grandmother, depriving them not only of the means of successful action, but of the means of action itself. Hence, we are depriving them of the very same basic goods that our friends are about to lose.

Now, we are certainly under an obligation to do what we can to save the lives of our friends, and, in cases of conflict, that obligation overrides duties to respect rights protecting goods that are less needed for agency. But, as has been pointed out here, the duty to rescue cannot override the duty to respect the right to the most basic form of well-being of our recipients. Regardless of the agent's motives, to torture an innocent child is a clear breach of the *PGC* and its emphasis on respect for the generic rights of our recipients. Hence, the *PGC* sets strict limits to what we are permitted to do to third parties in the course of rescue operations.

To clarify the picture of how we are to handle conflicts between rights, we should remind ourselves that while freedom and well-being are the generally necessary conditions of successful action, well-being is a complex feature, ranging from what the agent needs to initiate any action at all, to the goods that she needs to be successful in her pursuits. Gewirth has given a concise summary of well-being as a generic good of agency:

> Such well-being falls into a hierarchy of three different levels. *Basic well-being* consists in having the essential preconditions of action, such as life, physical integrity, mental equilibrium. *Nonsubtractive well-being* consists in having the general abilities and conditions needed for maintaining undiminished one's general level of purpose-fulfillment and one's capabilities for particular actions; examples are not being lied to or stolen from. *Additive well-being* consists in having the general abilities and conditions needed for increasing one's level of purpose-fulfillment and one's capabilities for particular actions; examples are education, self-esteem, and opportunities for acquiring wealth and income. (Gewirth, 1996, p. 14.)

Now, the hierarchy so established provides a criterion for solving conflicts between rights, namely, the *criterion of degrees of needfulness for action*, according to which that right takes precedence whose object is more needed for action (Gewirth, 1996, p. 45). One implication of this criterion is that the right to basic well-being in cases of conflict overrides the rights to non-subtractive and additive well-being. Another implication is that the right to basic well-being cannot be overridden by any other right (with the exception of cases of justified self-defence, in which the offender has forfeited his right not to have his basic well-being interfered with, should such interference be necessary to stop and rectify his abuses). And since the *PGC* prescribes that all agents should act in accord with the generic rights of their recipients, and since the right to basic well-being cannot be overridden by any other right, an agent can never be morally justified in violating the right to basic well-being of any of her recipients.

We could, of course, think of a case in which the agent is on board a tram which is speeding out of control, her choice being either to take the tram on to a track where it will kill one person, or to take it on to another track where it will kill ten persons. Here the agent is constrained by forces beyond her control in a way that makes it impossible for her not to play a causal role in the violation of other persons' rights to basic well-being. The only morally right thing for her to do is to minimize the harm to be inflicted and hence take the tram on to the track where one person will be killed.

Nagel's case is different, however. Here the agent is able to control whether or not her actions will violate anyone's right to basic well-being. If she refrains from twisting the child's arm and terrorizing the child's grandmother, she has acted in accord with their generic rights. If, on the other hand, as a consequence of the agent's respect for the rights of the child and the grandmother, her friends in the car will die, although the agent has done her best (within the limits set by the *PGC*) to save them, their deaths do not imply that the agent has violated their rights to basic well-being. She has fulfilled, to the best of her ability, her duty to rescue them. And since the *PGC* requires of her that she should act in accord with the generic rights of *all* of her recipients, the duty to rescue some persons, which is derived from their rights to basic well-being, cannot be invoked to set aside her duty not to violate that same right of another person. Hence, the agent is not morally justified in twisting the child's arm and terrorizing the child's grandmother for the sake of saving the lives of her injured friends, although she should do her best to save their lives within the limits set by the *PGC* (for instance, by trying to attract the attention of passing car-drivers, or trying to find a telephone booth from which to call for an ambulance, and so on).

In his analysis of the criterion of degrees of needfulness for action, Gewirth discusses an example that is rather similar to Nagel's, regarding whether it would not be right to remove one of a healthy person's kidneys or eyes in order to preserve the life or sight of another person. The possible justification for so doing would be a consequentialist interpretation of the criterion of degrees of needfulness for action: "For, after all, not being dead or blind is more needed for action than is having two kidneys or eyes" (1996, p. 50). In his conclusion Gewirth, however, rejects this kind of consequentialist reasoning, noting that when it comes to opposing one aspect of basic well-being to another, or one person's right to basic well-being to the same right of another person, there are limits to the application of the criterion of degrees of needfulness for action:

> These limits are especially set by the physical integrity which is an essential part of basic well-being. The policies cited above, removing healthy persons' kidneys or eyes to prevent the death or blindness of other persons, are attacks on the former persons' physical integrity. As such, they pose serious threats to their continued agency. Persons can indeed survive with one kidney or one eye; but, apart from their voluntary consent, the criterion of degrees of needfulness cannot justify such inflictions of basic harm. (Gewirth, 1996, p. 51.)

For the rest of the present book, when I refer to the objective self, I intend by that concept the objective agent-self, that is, an objective self which accepts deontological constraints as prescribed by the *PGC*. By adopting the idea of the objective agent-self, we are also enabled to solve the problems indicated at the beginning of this chapter. The process of objective detachment does not have to leave the agent bewildered and alienated. Instead it may point out to her that she shares with other agents the need for freedom and well-being, and that these generic goods of agency are also moral goods, in the sense that they are the objects of rationally justified right-claims. Moreover, the problem of finding a process of objective detachment that is neither too limited (and hence unable to transcend the prejudices of the agent's time and environment), nor too far removed from any human perspective (and hence unable to provide any moral guidance at all) can now be resolved. The sphere of agency transcends the limits of cultures and historical eras, while still pertaining to all human beings. You may be an agent without adhering to the prescriptions of a particular culture or religion. But you can never adhere to the prescriptions of any culture or religion without being an agent, since adhering to a prescription implies agency of one kind or another. Hence, the values generated by agency itself have a normative priority over the values generated within more specific contexts, such as a certain culture or religion.

By identifying with her objective agent-self, a person looks beyond the confines of the particularities of her time and place. At the same time she retains in focus those aspects of herself that she shares with other agents, i.e., being a person who by means of voluntary and purposive behaviour tries to realize her goals, and who in this process must claim rights to freedom and well-being as the generically necessary conditions of all successful action.

It is important to point out, however, that the objective agent-self does not confine itself to regulating interpersonal actions. It is also capable of forming a conception of the common good, to which subject we will now turn.

CHAPTER 6

The Common Good and Morality

The common good is always to be understood as the good of some *community*. Now, communities may vary as regards their extension. We can think of a range of associations, from the small-scale community of two friends or lovers, to the community of family and relatives, and further on to national communities, and transnational religious or ideological communties, ending with universal communities, including all human beings, or even all sentient beings. An influential argument holds that rationality indeed requires that we should take a maximally universal view of our communal attachments. Peter Singer, for instance, notes that

> The circle of altruism has broadened from the family and tribe to the nation and race, and we are beginning to recognize that our obligations extend to all human beings. The process should not stop there.... The only justifiable stopping place for the expansion of altruism is the point at which all whose welfare can be affected by our actions are included within the circle of altruism. This means that all beings with the capacity to feel pleasure or pain should be included; we can improve their welfare by increasing their pleasures and diminishing their pains. (Singer, 1981, p. 120.)

However, although I do not intend to deny that we have duties to non-human sentient beings (not to cause them unnecessary harm, for instance), I cannot endorse the view that we share a *community* with them. As I understand the concept of community, it requires a certain mutuality of rights and duties among its members. And such a mutuality does not exist between us and non-human animals. We may have duties to pigs not to treat them badly, but it does not make any sense to claim that pigs have duties to us. We cannot direct *moral* blame to pigs who, for instance, demolish our rose garden. Hence, there is no mutuality of rights and duties between us and pigs, and hence we do not share a community with them.

It could be objected here that we do not hold little children responsible for wreaking havoc upon our rose garden anymore than we do hold pigs responsible for their mischief. Does this mean that we do not share a community with our children? The answer is that it does not. Children have their place within a human morality since, given a normal course of development, they will become mature agents, sharing rights and duties with other humans. Likewise, persons who are deprived of their ability to participate in a mutually supportive framework of rights and duties, being the victims of accidents, illnesses, or the frailty of old age, remain members of our community, since we can recognize that it is a mere contingency that they do not share with us our capacity for moral agency. With pigs it is different, however. They are lacking the powers of moral agency not by accident, but by nature.

Moreover, we should distinguish between *morally contingent* and *morally necessary* communities. A morally contingent community is a community the existence of which is not morally required for the protection of the generic rights (although it may be morally permitted as being at least consistent with the *PGC*). A family is a typical morally contingent community, in the sense that persons are not under a moral obligation to get married and have children, but they are free to do so, provided that they do not violate each other's or anybody else's rights to freedom and well-being in the process. Likewise, labour unions, political parties, and religious congregations constitute morally contingent communities in the sense indicated here.

A morally necessary community, on the other hand, is a community the existence of which is morally required for the protection of the generic rights. The civic community, i.e., the community of citizens of a territorial state, is a necessary community, to the extent that it provides legal protection and enforcement of the generic rights for all its members. It is important to note that the civic community is not just any political community, but a community of *citizens*. Any political community may fulfil at least some of the basic requirements of the *PGC*, simply by being a minimal state which protects its subjects from being murdered, assaulted, or having their property stolen from them. But it is only a civic community that is also able to fulfil the political implications of the freedom requirement of the *PGC*, by granting its members the status of citizens, thereby conferring on them the right to participation in the rule of their community, including the civic rights to vote and to stand as candidates in political elections:

> As involving the civil liberties, the right to political democracy is an application of the PGC's right to freedom. The PGC's protection of this right requires that each person be left free to engage in any action or transaction according to his unforced choice so long as he does not coerce or harm other persons. These protected actions include speaking, publishing, and associating with others, so that, as a matter of constitutional requirement, each person is able, if he chooses, to discuss, criticize, and vote for or against the government and to work actively with other persons or groups of various sizes to further his political objectives. (Gewirth, 1996, p. 315.)

Accordingly, a civic community is a community of self-rule, in the sense that its members obey only laws to which they themselves or their freely elected representatives have consented. But it is important to note that the civic community does not always coincide with the political community. That is, in a political community (i.e., an independent territorial state) where only some people have the civic rights (the males, those who possess a certain wealth, those who belong to a certain ethnic or religious group, and so on), it is only these people who are included in the civic community. The other members of the political community are subjects, but not citizens. Historically speaking, civic communities in the Western world have often begun as such relatively small élite communities, and gradually evolved to include all members of their respective political communities. And, in line with the universalism of the *PGC*, such a development is indeed morally required. All persons have the right to be citizens, i.e., members of a civic community, since they share with the members of the élite the quality of being agents with rights to freedom and well-being.

It is important in this context that we do not conflate the moral necessity of the civic community as a form for politically organizing a state, with the historical contingency pertaining to existing political communities, regarding features such as their territorial extension and ethnic composition. The *PGC* makes it mandatory that all political communities should also be civic communities. However, the *PGC* does not make it mandatory that a particular political community C should exist, or that C should have this particular territorial extension or that kind of ethnic composition. It is not morally necessary that Ruritania exists, but if it exists it should be a civic community.

Moreover, it is important that we keep in mind the distinction (mentioned in chapter 4) between positive and normative conceptions of the common good, that is, between conceptions of the common good that, as a matter of fact, are *believed* to be justified by the members of some community, and conceptions that *are* justified, according to valid criteria of reasoning. The dedicated members of a Nazi community, or of an Apartheid community, or of the community of Pol Pot and the Khmer Rouge, will entertain conceptions of the common good that are very different from the common good of the civic community described above. But a conception of the common good should not be accepted as morally justified, just because it happens to be endorsed by the members of some community. Their conclusions regarding the common good may be based on factual or logical errors. Hence, we need an independent criterion of moral rightness in order to pronounce on the various moral aspects of different conceptions of the common good. The argument from agency and its generally necessary conditions provides such an independent criterion, in the form of the *PGC*.

Hence, we are able to claim that the conceptions of the common good advanced by the Nazis, the Apartheid racists, and the Khmer Rouge are morally unjustified, since they reject the idea that all agents have rights to freedom and well-being. However, the fact that some conceptions of the common good are morally unjustified does not mean that they cannot be causally productive of the courage of conviction. On the contrary, the fanaticism of a committed Nazi or a committed Khmer Rouge is very much dependent upon their identification with their respective community, and on their sense of moral responsibility for its preservation. Hence, while the fact that an agent is able to confront her fear of personal transience out of a sense of moral responsibility and a commitment to the common good of her community certainly implies that she possesses the courage of conviction, it does not imply that her sense of moral responsibility, nor the common good to which she is committed, are justified.

That the *PGC* does not make the existence of particular states morally mandatory does not, of course, imply that the *PGC* is indifferent as regards the means whereby states actually come into existence or cease to exist. The creation as well as the preservation or dissolution of states constitute actions, and all actions can be morally evaluated as being either in conformity with or in breach of the prescriptions of the *PGC*.

Moreover, in line with the universalism of the *PGC*, a civic community must not promote the generic rights of its own citizens at the expense of the generic rights of members of other political communities. Hence, "civic egoism" is ruled out. Examples of such egoism could be the exploitation of cheap labour in countries where labour unions are prohibited and civic rights are not respected, as well as the introduction of import regulations which deny producers in the third world access to the world market, for the sake of protecting domestic producers. In both these cases, the additive good of domestic wealth is bought at the expense of the workers of less fortunate communities. (This does not mean, however, that the opposite extreme, "civic self-denial", is to be preferred. The *PGC* prescribes that we should act in accord with the generic rights of our recipients *as well as of ourselves*. Hence, just as a person who cannot swim is not required to jump in the ocean to save a drowning man and risk his own life in the process, so a civic community is not supposed to starve its own citizens in order to alleviate global starvation.) Positively speaking, any civic community should encourage and support the creation and preservation of civic communities at a global level. The governments as well as the individual citizens of civic communities should take an active interest in the democratization and social development of other political communities. Hence, the right to form labour unions should be supported globally, even if that means that consumers in the rich world will have to pay more for imported goods. Likewise, free trade should be encouraged, even if that means stronger competition for domestic enterprises.

It should also be noted that, although the universalist morality defended here rules out nationalist chauvinism and collective egoism, it will endorse a certain form of *civic pride*. Accordingly, citizens are justified in being proud of the contributions made, domestically as well as internationally, by their civic community as a whole or by individual fellow citizens, to increase the awareness of the importance of the agency-related rights to freedom and well-being, as well as to the institutionalization and implementation of these rights.

Moreover, civic communities should cooperate with each other for the purpose of giving collective support, including military assistance, to individual civic communities that are threatened by external or internal hostility. Support should also be given to groups within political communities who, in opposition to dictatorial and repressive governments, try to transform their country into a civic community. Support should not be extended, however, to groups who do not have a civic community as their end, but rather a different form of despotism, such as a fundamentalist theocratic government.

Hence, given the instrumental necessity of the civic community for the protection of the generic rights, and given also the universalism of the *PGC*, the common good can be seen to have two morally justified dimensions. The common good in its *civic* dimension is that our particular political community shall (continue to) be a civic community, in which we, the members of this particular political community, are citizens with civic rights. The common good in its *universal* dimension is that we, the agents of the world, shall have our generic rights to freedom and well-being universally protected.

And, to the extent that we are rational agents, being aware of our generic rights, our sense of moral responsibility will enjoin us to support the common good in both of its dimensions. This sense of moral responsibility for the civic and universal dimensions of the common good is what motivates a morally justified courage of conviction.

While the civic dimension refers to a particularized "we", namely, a certain group of citizens or potential citizens of a particular political community, the universal dimension refers to a universal "we", namely, the inclusive group of all agents. And since a person cannot be a citizen without also being an agent, the common good of a particular community of citizens must be consistent with the common good of all agents. Moreover, as the civic rights of the members of a particular civic community should be seen as an application of the generic rights of all agents, and not as an independent moral domain, it should be evident that the common good of a particular civic community cannot contradict the common good of all agents without depriving itself of its moral justification. In fact, it may well be their recognition of freedom and well-being as objects of the universal common good of all agents that convinces members of a certain political community that their present condition is intolerable, and prompts them to demand civic rights for themselves. (Think of, for instance, the French declaration of rights of 1789, with its reference to the "rights of man and of the citizen"; see the discussion of this text in Rials, 1988.)

Moreover, it is important to note that we may contribute to the common good not only by participating in collective undertakings, such as the military defence of our country, but also by assisting particular individuals against threats to their freedom or well-being (for instance, by protecting a person from being robbed or beaten up by street thugs). When the common good is conceived of as the maintenance of certain rights of all persons (whether in their capacity as citizens of a particular community, or as members of an imagined universal community of agents), such contributions to the protection of the generic goods of individual persons will also count as contributions to the common good.

It is also important to note that the view of the common good that is defended here does not imply the view endorsed by various communitarian philosophers, that the individual is "embedded" in a particular social context and hence simply "inherits" a socio-historical identity as well as various obligations to the communities of which that social context is made up. On the contrary, the conception of the common good developed here assumes that individuals are *agents*, and that they are capable of making a critical assessment of the traditions and values of their communities (that is, unless they are prevented from doing so by oppressive social conditions which themselves constitute violations of the generic rights of all agents). The fact that a certain conception of the common good is actually held to be justified within a particular community, and the fact that individuals living in that community are likely to be influenced by that conception, do not imply that the conception in question is morally justified. Nor does it imply that the members of that community should be loyal to its conception of the common good, just because it is the conception of *their* community.

Hence, our argument presupposes a distinction between *causal* and *normative* theses regarding the common good, a distinction which seems to be ignored by philosophers of the communitarian brand. For instance, Alasdair MacIntyre, who finds it as easy to dismiss the idea of human rights as it is to dismiss talk of witches and unicorns – "every attempt to give good reasons for believing that there *are* such rights has failed" (MacIntyre, p. 69) – argues from the causal hypothesis that the good for an individual is determined by her social identity to the normative conclusion that this socially determined good *is* the good for that individual:

> [I]t is not just that different individuals live in different social circumstances; it is also that we all approach our own circumstances as bearers of a particular social identity. I am someone's son or daughter, someone else's cousin or uncle; I am a citizen of this or that city, a member of this or that guild or profession; I belong to this clan, that tribe, this nation. Hence what is good for me has to be the good for one who inhabits these roles. As such, I inherit from the past of my family, my city, my tribe, my nation, a variety of debts, inheritances, rightful expectations and obligations. These constitute the given of my life, my moral starting point.... For the story of my life is always embedded in the story of those

communities from which I derive my identity. I am born with a past; and to try to cut myself off from that past, in the individualist mode, is to deform my present relationships. The possession of an historical identity and the possession of a social identity coincide....What I am, therefore, is in key part what I inherit, a specific past that is present to some degree in my present. I find myself part of a history and that is generally to say, whether I like it or not, whether I recognize it or not, one of the bearers of a tradition. (MacIntyre, pp. 220–221.)

Now, in addition to the logical problem of deriving moral norms from social facts, we have reason to question the causal part of MacIntyre's argument. Even if it seems reasonable to assume that the beliefs of individuals regarding the common good are *influenced* by the prevailing views within their communities, it does not follow that their beliefs regarding the common good are *determined* by these views. Even prevailing views within a particular community are subjected to challenges, not only in the form of external influences, but also in the form of differing interpretations within the community in question:

> After all, even in traditional societies a person occupies more than one social role, and the social institutions that define these roles serve as varied paths by which culturally shaped patterns of belief and behavior are transmitted. These paths for the transmission of culture ultimately generate a wide variety of "positions" or perspectives, both inside and outside any culture, from which it is possible to reflect on the elements of that culture.... Men and women, for instance, may develop different understandings of central cultural phenomena.... Differences in material well-being, in political or religious authority, even in age, will be linked to varied and sometimes quite elaborate overlapping patterns of normative expectations about behavior. (Moody-Adams, p. 68.)

Hence, a person's social context will admit of more diversity and room for conflicting views than the communitarian account seems to imply. However, the important thing to remember here is that the conception of the common good that is defended in this study is a normative one, and that its justification is not contingent upon any causal thesis regarding how people actually come to conceive of the common good, due to various aspects of their different social contexts.

When an agent confronts her fear of personal transience out of a sense of moral responsibility for the common good in either its civic or its universal dimension, she manifests a morally justified courage of conviction. (This is not meant to deny that agents who confront their fear of personal transience for the sake of the common good of, let us say, a fundamentalist and theocratic political order, are courageous, too. But it is meant to imply that their courage, motivated by a cause which is inconsistent with the generic rights of all agents, as prescribed by the *PGC*, is not *morally justified*.) And in a political community dominated by a powerful and intolerant aristocratic or theocratic élite, it may indeed require courage to advance the cause of civic rights, by, for instance, publishing articles or books in defence of such rights, or by organizing demonstrations against the present rulers. Even in a community where civic rights are officially recognized, it may take courage to demand their practical implementation, as was shown by the reactions in the American South to the campaign in support of the rights of coloured people headed by Martin Luther King in the 1960s. Likewise, it takes courage to support a civic community against the armed aggression of non-democratic neighbouring states, or against the armed attacks of non-democratic domestic forces. (Hitler's Germany may exemplify the first kind of threat, at least from the point of view of the democratic countries of Europe during the 1930s and 1940s, while Franco's rebellion in Spain in 1936 may exemplify the second kind of threat to civic rule.)

Moreover, just as her recognition of the value of the civic community may provide an agent with the motivation necessary to confront her fear of personal transience in that aspect which is related to the fear of dying, so can that same value provide her with the motivation necessary to cope with the fear of meaninglessness. She might, for instance, dedicate herself to the ideal of *enlightened citizenship*, which includes acquiring knowledge not only of current social and political issues but also of the political history of her community. Thereby she will enable herself to make a responsible use of her civic rights, and to make the most of her citizenship, utilizing a perspective on current affairs that is not narrowly confined to recent developments but is capable of connecting and comparing these developments to the achievements of previous generations of members of her political community. Hence, the agent will enable herself to avoid both an unduly romanticized view of a supposedly idyllic past and the naive kind of evolutionary optimism which assumes that later stages of development necessarily must be superior to earlier stages, and that we therefore have nothing to learn from history. She will also be able to reaffirm her identification with her civic community by recognizing that the civic rights that she is presently enjoying are the outcome of a long struggle for political freedom, involving the courageous efforts of previous generations of members of her political community. Seeing herself as a beneficiary of these historical efforts rather than as a self-sufficient individual, she may have her sense of moral responsibility for the common good of her civic community further strengthened. At the same time, the very project of acquiring the knowledge required for enlightened citizenship will be meaningful, as it can be experienced as a contribution to the common good in its own right.

As a consequence of her assuming responsibility for the common good in its civic dimension, the agent may also choose an occupation that is productive not only in the sense that it enables her to support herself, but also in the sense that it contributes to the ideal of a civic community. Since a civic community requires educated and informed citizens who can make a responsible use of their civic rights, it may indeed be meaningful from the point of view of the common good in its civic dimension to take up a career in teaching or in journalism. And since the exercise of civic rights requires good health and a safe neighbourhood, meaning will also attach to professions like those of the doctor and the police officer. By a similar indirect line of argument many other kinds of work can be shown to be meaningful, since they contribute, within the limits set by the rights to freedom and well-being of producers as well as of consumers, in various way to the flourishing of a civic community by providing its individual members with goods and services that they need for the realization of their various conceptions of a good life. Likewise, meaning can be provided from serving the common good in its universal dimension, by, for instance, volunteering to be a relief worker in a poor country, or by participating in an international peace-keeping force in a community plagued by civil war, or by dedicating oneself to the pursuit of scientific or philosophical knowledge, thereby contributing to an increase in human understanding generally.

However, it is important to note that for the agent to be able to derive meaning from these forms of contribution to the common good, she must also take a personal interest in the work done. A person who takes up teaching just for the sake of serving the common good but who hates everything that comes with the job (such as having a lot of noisy kids around) is not likely to be successful at her work, nor is she likely to find her contribution meaningful. Accordingly, the willingness to contribute to the common good should be accompanied by a self-knowledge on the agent's part, whereby she can give her contribution a content that suits her talents.

We may conclude, then, that the courage of conviction can be given a moral justification when it is applied in the service of either the civic or the universal dimensions of the common good. Moreover, by identifying with our objective agent-selves we are able to derive not only a universally valid moral principle from the generic features of agency, but also to provide ourselves with the motivation necessary to act in accordance with it, even in the face of our fear of personal transience. Hence, in the process of identifying with the prescriptions of the objective agent-self, we will acquire a sense of moral responsibility which prompts us to stand up for the generic rights of individual persons as well as for the common good in the form of institutional arrangements for the maintenance of these rights locally (within a particular civic community) as well as universally. In this process of objective detachment, the common good of our civic community, as well as the common good of all agents, can be perceived by us to be indeed *goods*, and goods *for us*.

CHAPTER 7

Combining the Two Forms of Courage

In the preceding chapters we have outlined the basic framework of a theory of courage. We have related courage to the agent's ability to confront fear, and we have distinguished two forms of courage, the courage of creativity and the courage of conviction. In the remainder of the present study, we will clarify this idea of courage by confronting it with a series of questions. These questions concern the relationship between the two forms of courage, as well as the relationship between them and dispositions such as heroism and prudence.

The first question focuses on the alleged importance to an agent's having a good life of her possessing both the courage of creativity and the courage of conviction. As it seems possible to have one form of courage without the other, we might ask ourselves if we really need them both. Perhaps the one is more important for an agent's good life than the other. Perhaps we can do without one form of courage and still enjoy a fully satisfying life. If this is the case, we might well save ourselves the trouble of inculcating in ourselves both forms of courage.

Let us illuminate this problem by studying the historical cases of two persons who each possessed one of the two forms of courage, but not the other. American explorer Meriwether Lewis (1774–1809) here exemplifies the courage of creativity, while French revolutionary politician Maximilien Robespierre (1758–94) provides an illustration of the courage of conviction.

Lewis

On 15 April 1805, just a week after he and his men had left Fort Mandan, Meriwether Lewis passed the farthest point upstream on the Missouri known by him to have been reached by white men. Now he and his long-time friend William Clark and their expedition were heading into the unknown, looking for a possible water passage connecting the Missouri with the Columbia, and so joining America's West to her East. Having been assigned this explorative mission by President Thomas Jefferson, the prospect of danger and hardship did not seem to burden Lewis:

> He was entering a heart of darkness. Deserts, mountains, great cataracts, warlike Indian tribes – he could not imagine them, because no American had ever seen them. But, far from causing apprehension or depression, the prospect brought out his fullest talents. He knew that from now on, until he reached the Pacific and returned, he would be making history. He was exactly what Jefferson wanted him to be, optimistic, prudent, alert to all that was new about him, and able to describe the flora and fauna, the native inhabitants, and the skies above with scientific measurement. His health was excellent. His ambition was boundless. His determination was complete. He could not, would not, contemplate failure. (Ambrose, p. 216.)

Meriwether Lewis seems in many ways to have been an excellent commander of men. Although he was of an impulsive disposition, he was usually able to control himself and, adding prudence to courage, to avoid falling victim to rashness. This self-restraint was manifested on one occasion in which Lewis observed from land how his crew lost control of the white pirogue carrying his journals, maps, instruments, and other important objects. A sudden squawl had turned the vessel, and the panic-stricken man at the helm, instead of turning the bow into the wind let the pirogue turn with the wind, which drew the brace of the sail out of the hands of the men. Lewis feared the pirogue would go under.

> Reacting instinctively, he dropped his rifle, threw aside his shot pouch, and began tearing off his coat. His idea was to swim unencumbered out to the pirogue to save what he could. But before he dived into the river, "I recollected the folly of the attempt I was

about to make." The waves were high, the boat was three hundred yards away, the water was excessively cold, and the current strong. "There was a hundred to one but what I should have paid the forfit of my life for the madness of my project," he wrote that evening in his journal. (Ambrose, p. 225; spelling here as well as in the following quotations as in the original)

Lewis' courage was equal parts determination and optimism. His optimism was not of the kind that predicts of the world that all things are, as a matter of fact, going well and will continue to do so. Rather, it was an attitude of positive possibilism, anticipating the possibility of a good outcome. And this attitude manifested itself in a capacity for positive planning on Lewis' part. On 26 May 1805, he pondered in his journal the hardships ahead, as he and his men were about to cross the Rocky Mountains, concluding:

> As I have always held it a crime to anticipate evils I will believe it a good comfortable road untill I am conpelled to beleive differently. (Ambrose, p. 227.)

This optimistic confidence is obviously a good quality in a commander of an expedition exploring unknown and unmapped territories. Meriwether Lewis also seems to have been able to inspire his men with his own capacity for constructive creativity at critical moments. On one occasion one of his men, Private Windsor, slipped on a narrow walkway and was about to fall down into a precipice of ninety feet, his right hand, arm, and leg already over the edge. Windsor cried out for help, almost overwhelmed by fear. Lewis, who just had saved himself from slipping down that same precipice, managed to calm Windsor down, while at the same time telling him what to do to get back on firm ground:

> He assured Windsor he was in no danger, then told him to take the knife out of his belt with his right hand and dig a hole with it in the face of the bluff to receive his right foot.
>
> Windsor did as instructed, and with his foot in the hole was able to raise himself to his knees. Lewis told him to take off his

moccasins (the wet leather was more slippery than bare feet) and crawl forward on his hands and knees, taking care to hold the knife in one hand and his rifle in the other. "This he happily effected and escaped." (Ambrose, p. 233.)

Lewis combined agency-related optimism regarding the unknown with determination regarding the obstacles and dangers he knew would confront him. Being forced to take canoes and baggage by land to bypass the Great Falls of Missouri, Lewis confined himself to the dryly realistic comment, that "[g]ood or bad we must make the portage" (Ambrose, 242). And when he realized that there is no all-water connection between the Missouri and the Pacific, and that he would have to cross the Rocky Mountains, he took comfort in the information he got from an Indian chief, that the Nez Percés regularly crossed the mountains in the other direction to hunt buffalo in the Missouri district.

> What route did they use? Lewis asked. It was to the north, the chief answered, "but added that the road was a very bad one as he had been informed by them and that they had suffered excessively with hunger on the rout being obliged to subsist for many days on berries alone as there was no game in that part of the mountains which were broken rockey and so thickly covered with timber that they could scarcely pass."
>
> Far from being downcast by such a description, Lewis was encouraged. "My rout was instantly settled in my own mind," he wrote. "I felt perfectly satisfyed that if the Indians could pass these mountains with their women and Children, that we could also pass them." (Ambrose, p. 272.)

Lewis manifested the same confident courage on another potentially dangerous occasion, when he had to convince Shoshone chief Cameahwait that he was not about to betray the Shoshones to the Blackfeet. By deliberately making himself and his men vulnerable to the Shoshones he succeeded in securing Cameahwait's trust:

[H]e gave Cameahwait his rifle and told him that if the Blackfeet were around he could use it to defend himself, "that for my own part I was not affraid to die and if I deceived him he might make what uce of the gun he thought proper or in other words that he might shoot me." Lewis had his men give up their rifles too, "which seemed to inspire them [the Indians] with more confidence". (Ambrose, p. 276.)

In this context it is important to note that Lewis' explicit statement, that he is not afraid to die, does not necessarily mean that he has confronted the fear of personal transience in the sense relevant to the courage of conviction. Lewis' decision to make himself and his men vulnerable to the Shoshones is not motivated by a sense of moral responsibility. He does not presume that he is morally obligated to take this risk. Instead, he seems to have made an estimation of the risks at hand, according to which the likelihood that he and his men would fall victim to a Shoshone attack should decrease rather than increase if they handed over their weapons to the Shoshones. This, however, is an example of the courage of creativity and an application of the principle of constructive creativity. Lewis is not acting out of a moral conviction here. He is simply trying to make the most of a difficult situation, opting for that line of action which seems to offer his expedition the best chances of a successful outcome.

However, Lewis' optimistic confidence very much depended on the context. It seems as if the extreme conditions of the expedition functioned to ward off a depressive streak in his character by recurrently propelling him into action. Confronted with obstacles, be they the hardships brought on by the wilderness or the hostility of Indians, he was able to mobilize his experience and skills in a constructive way. But left to himself with no imminent danger to deal with, he was prone to sink into an introspective mood that generated a pessimism about his own capacities. On his thirty-first birthday (18 August 1805) he complained in his journal that he "had as yet done but little, very little indeed, to further the hapiness [sic] of the human race, or to advance the information of the succeeding generation". He criticized himself for "the many hours I have spent in indolence" and resolved that in the future he would "live for *mankind,* as I have heretofore lived *for myself*" (Ambrose, p. 280).

Indolence or, more neutrally, lack of purpose, seemed to be what Lewis feared the most. He was a talented man, but he needed a motivating force to mobilize his capabilities. Jefferson seemed to have understood how to get Lewis going, and once the Lewis and Clark expedition was afoot, the vast wilderness itself provided Lewis with a powerful impetus to action. To get the expedition up and down rivers and across mountains, providing food and shelter for its members, warding off angry grizzly bears, and making contacts with Indians, gave little room for "indolence". And, as Ambrose notices, Lewis "always was happiest when proceeding" (p. 357).

However, once the expedition was successfully concluded (late in 1806) and Lewis had returned to civilization, his life deteriorated rapidly. Jefferson had rewarded him with the post of governor of the Territory of Louisiana late in February 1807. Lewis does not seem to have known what to do with this assignment. Although being on the government's pay-roll from the time of his appointment, he did not arrive at his office in St. Louis until early March 1808. Meanwhile he seems to have devoted himself to heavy drinking and (unsuccessful) romantic adventures. As a governor he got involved in speculations in land and in the fur trade. His plan seems to have been to organize a private fur company, paid by public funds, and with a regional monopoly on the fur trade (Ambrose, p. 461). Lewis was never to benefit from this scheme, however. Heavily in debt, and with a new administration in Washington (Jefferson's second term ended in March 1809) that was not prepared to accept some unauthorized drafts that Lewis had made on the government, he was facing personal bankruptcy and public disgrace. Constant drinking aggravated his mood, and on 11 October 1809 he shot himself twice and died a few hours later. In these final hours of pain he seems to have been anxious to preserve the image of his own courage:

> I am no coward; but I am so strong, [it is] so hard to die. (Ambrose, p. 475.)

Jefferson, who knew Lewis well from the time the latter served as his personal secretary and lived with him in the President's House (later called the White House) in Washington, was aware of Lewis' mood swings. He seems to have been the first to suggest the above idea of the balancing effects of the expedition on Lewis' depressions:

> While he lived with me in Washington, I observed at times sensible depressions of mind, but knowing their constitutional source [referring to Lewis' father, who also seems to have suffered from depression], I estimated their course by what I had seen in the family. During his Western expedition the constant exertion which that required of all the faculties of body & mind, suspended these distressing affections; but after his establishment at St. Louis in sedentary occupations they returned upon him with redoubled vigor, and began seriously to alarm his friends. (Ambrose, p. 477.)

Meriwether Lewis was no coward, as he himself said, but his courage was that of creativity rather than that of conviction. He was faithful to the task assigned to him even in the face of severe hardship. But he seems to have lacked a normative conviction of his own to direct his courage and to preserve his moral integrity, which became evident as he got immersed in state politics. As long as he was given objectives to accomplish that required continuous efforts to ward off dangers and to confront more or less unexpected adversities, he was at his best. He manifested a constructive creativity and a capacity for positive planning which ensured his expedition of a successful outcome. However, as he himself complained on one occasion, he lacked a greater purpose in his life, a purpose which could provide his life with a moral meaning and himself with a lasting self-respect. He was excellent in carrying out Jefferson's assignment, but he was a failure when left to himself with comparatively extensive freedom to act according to his own inclinations. Indeed, it seems as if his courage of creativity, not being constrained by the external standards inherent in the courage of conviction, made him reckless and too confident in his own capacity for success. An inflated self-confidence and a lack of the moral integrity and self-respect related to self-transcendent values and projects of meaning may have combined to bring Lewis down.

Robespierre

An interesting comparison here is the case of Maximilien Robespierre, who possessed a well-documented moral integrity as well as a courage of conviction. At the same time he seems to have been deficient in the courage of creativity, as he was generally pessimistic about his prospects, envisaging himself as the constant victim of intrigue and persecution. Robespierre, unlike Lewis, knew what to do when in power, as he was guided by definite moral goals. However, his lack of a positive outlook made him, also unlike Lewis, vulnerable in times of crisis, as he tended to panic and advocate extreme measures, rather than looking for pragmatic solutions and making the best of things as they were.

Already at the very beginning of revolutionary politics, as he was campaigning in the elections to the Estates General in the spring of 1789, Robespierre formulated two themes that he was later to repeat many times throughout his political career: that political action should be understood as the practice of moral principles, and that the righteous must be prepared to suffer for their convictions. In this context he also explicitly refers to courage, as a necessary virtue of anyone who is to take up the cause of liberty and justice:

> Is it to subject the generous impulses of lofty spirits to timid caution, concerned only with personal well-being, that the Eternal Founder of human society has endowed men's hearts with a generous feeling that sends them without hesitation to the help of the oppressed, with courage unshaken in the midst of dangers, calm in the eye of the storm, in a word, with all those divine virtues that make them worthy to sacrifice their all for the glory and happiness of their country?...
>
> Who is the citizen who, if his enchanting aspirations for the relief of humanity and the triumph of the nation were disappointed, would complain of being destined to suffer with it, of being spared the misfortune of surviving its ruin? (Quoted in Hampson, pp. 41–42.)

While Robespierre's strength may have been his moral integrity (he was not named "the Incorruptible" for nothing), his weakness was his alarmist tendencies and his readiness to see "plots" and "conspiracies" everywhere. His often sweeping accusations alienated many of his colleagues, and when they reacted by ridiculing him, or by open opposition to his moralized view of politics, this was taken by Robespierre as further evidence of their corruption. Already in his first years as an active politician (in the National Assembly, 1789–91), he was known for his ability to spot conspiracies that might endanger the Revolution:

> When the Genoese put in an optimistic claim for the recovery of Corsica, that was an English plot. When Spain requested French support in a colonial quarrel with England, under the terms of the Franco-Spanish alliance, that was a royalist plot to get France involved in a war. The Avignon business was a plot to provide a safe base for counter-revolutionaries. The Ministers were plotting to rig the municipal elections. Peasants who burned châteaux were the tools of secret agents who were trying to discredit the revolution. Sometimes he convinced the deputies but on other occasions his suspicions were a source of ridicule. 'M. de Robespierre, as usual, spoke of plots, conspiracies, etc., etc.,' wrote Duquesnoy, a fellow-deputy in January 1790. Two months later the *Mercure de France* said that he had 'once again enlarged on the plots and conspiracies of which he alone held the secret'. (Hampson, p. 64.)

As Hampson points out in his biography, Robespierre's constant detection of new conspiracies was "not merely a matter of his credulity, but of his pessimism" (p. 65). Robespierre found it difficult to believe that justice and liberty would prevail without the interference of Providence, the blessings of which he often invoked in his speeches.

> From his pessimistic viewpoint, the survival of the revolution through so many perils and betrayals was only explicable as the work of Providence. He said this over and over again from 1790 onwards. In July 1794 he personalised it to the extent of claiming

that Providence had saved him from assassination. Besides protecting him, Providence would offer a final consolation in the event of failure: death was 'a safe and precious asylum that Providence has reserved for *vertu*'. (Hampson, p. 181.)

And since he identified himself with the self-transcendent cause of justice and liberty, he came to view attacks on his person as attacks on the values he stood for, and vice versa. Add to this that he was easily offended. This was certainly to a large extent an effect of his being subjected to the "most vicious calumny and misrepresentation" (Hampson, p. 66) in the press from the very beginning of his political career. Another reason, more in the psychoanalytical tradition, for his touchiness in questions regarding moral integrity, would be found in his childhood years. Maximilien's mother died when he was six, and his father abandoned the children (Maximilien, Charlotte, Henriette, and Augustin), leaving them to be brought up by their maternal grandparents. Maximilien, being the eldest of the children, would have been under great pressure to prove himself worthy of other people's trust, given his father's irresponsibility, and given the vicious tradition of visiting the sins of the fathers on their children. Hence his early development of a strongly principled mind and a stern moral integrity. At the same time, the erratic behaviour of his father is likely to have made it hard for Maximilien to develop an attitude of confident trust regarding other people. It might also have contributed to his pessimism which later in his life often manifested itself in times of crisis. This psychological explanation of Robespierre's moralism is developed by Max Gallo, who summarizes his thesis in the following words:

> Là où il y avait irresponsabilité, insouciance, rejet des principes, le sens du devoir, la gravité, la vertu s'imposent. Maximilien n'a pas d'autres choix psychologiques. [Where there had been irresponsibility, carelessness, and rejection of principles, sense of duty, seriousness, and virtue impose themselves. Maximilien does not have any other psychological choice.] (Gallo, pp. 25–26.)

A German member of the Jacobin club by the name of Oelsner, who met Robespierre socially, thought that "he had the strength of will of a great man but that he lacked courage, political sense and knowledge of the world" (Hampson, p. 82). Now, if Robespierre lacked courage it would have been the courage of creativity, which left him vulnerable to pessimism and a lack of self-confidence, as when on 12 June 1793 he told the Jacobins that

> If we were united, if we were agreed on principles, every *patriote* would have an energy and a confidence that he doesn't have now. So far as I am concerned, I declare my own insufficiency. I have no longer the vigour it needs to fight the intrigues of the aristocracy. Worn out by four years of arduous and fruitless toil, I feel that my physical and moral faculties are far from the level needed for a great revolution and I declare that I shall resign. (Quoted in Hampson, p. 152.)

Likewise, it was suggested by at least one of Robespierre's contemporaries (a man called Tissot) that the decision to have his revolutionary rival Danton executed was motivated by fear rather than by hatred: "Robespierre did not want Danton's death, but he was easily frightened" (quoted in Hampson, p. 254). The pessimism of Robespierre is also included in a hostile memoir, written some time after Robespierre's death, by Laurent Lecointre, member of the National Convention (the elected parliament of the French republic 1792–95):

> He was always bringing us his worries, his suspicions, his touchy manner and his political moodiness; he was only concerned with personalities and only proposed arrests and dealt with factions, the press and the revolutionary tribunal. Useless in government, useless in war, with never a point of view to put forward or a report to present, he spent his time undermining our courage, despairing of the salvation of the nation, speaking about his slanderers and assassins; his favourite expressions were: *all is lost; there is no ressource; I can no longer see anyone to save us*. (Quoted in Hampson, pp. 271–272.)

However, Robespierre certainly possessed the courage of conviction, in the form of a preparedness to die for self-transcendent ends. In fact, Robespierre cultivated in his speeches a view of patriotic martyrdom, which was not only the outcome of pessimistic brooding, but also signals a certain heroic attitude:

> To what worthier end could one devote one's life? It is not enough to find death at the hands of tyrants; one must have deserved it ... If the first champions of liberty must be its martyrs they must carry tyranny itself to their tombs. The death of a great man must awaken the sleeping peoples and its price must be the welfare of the world. (Quoted in Hampson, p. 104.)

And although he may have despaired about his own abilities, he was never in doubt about the values he was fighting for. Robespierre's particular blend of patriotism, infused with universalist moral ideals of justice and liberty, is to him a civic religion, justifying and motivating every kind of personal self-sacrifice:

> O my country! If it had been my fate to be born in a distant foreign land I should have addressed continual prayers to heaven for your prosperity ... I am French, I am one of your representatives ... O sublime people, receive the sacrifice of my entire being! (Quoted in Hampson, p. 159.)

In his speech on the principles of political morality that should guide the domestic policy of the Convention (5 February 1794) Robespierre made it clear that "[i]n the system of the French Revolution, whatever is immoral is bad politics, what corrupts is counter-revolutionary" (quoted in Hampson, p. 160). Hence, the patriotism he advocated was also a programme for moral regeneration, aiming at substituting

> principles for conventions, duties for social obligations, the empire of reason for the tyranny of fashion, contempt of vice for contempt of misfortune, pride for insolence, greatness of soul for vanity, love of glory for love of money, good people for the right society,

merit for intrigue, genius for wit, truth for show, the charms of true happiness for the satiety of lust, the greatness of man for the pettiness of the great, a magnanimous, powerful and happy people for an agreeable, frivolous and miserable one; in other words, all the virtues and miracles of the Republic for all the ridiculous vices of monarchy. (Quoted in Hampson, p. 160.)

In the end, however, Robespierre found himself increasingly isolated also within the Committee of Public Safety (which functioned as a *de facto* revolutionary government in the year 1793–94). The revolutionary terror had created a climate of suspicion and fear, culminating with the prairial law of 10 June 1794, which stated the death penalty for all "enemies of the people", a category which was sufficiently vague to include "almost any expression of criticism, pessimism or immorality" (Hampson, p. 275). While the terror escalated, it became also increasingly difficult to dismantle it, as the friends of its earlier victims were likely to revenge themselves on retired ex-terrorists. Robespierre had hinted vaguely at a possible need for a further purge of the Convention, which caused alarm among those who felt themselves implicated, and brought about a confrontation in the Committee of Public Safety, as several members of that committee found it ill advised to provoke the Convention. Robespierre felt himself isolated, and told his colleagues so: "I see clearly enough that I am alone." Then he accused them of protecting his enemies in the Convention who were out to destroy him. Billaud-Varenne, another member of the Committee of Public Safety, in his turn accused Robespierre of planning to guillotine the Convention, upon which Robespierre is said to have burst into tears and left the room (Hampson, p. 278).

When Robespierre finally decides to confront his enemies by denouncing them to the Convention, he in fact signs his own death-warrant. Seemingly without any tactical sense, Robespierre on 26 July 1794 made a sweeping attack on members of the most important political committees, which could only increase the determination of all those who felt themselves implicated to join together and try to get rid of him. Robespierre's conclusion was very significative for a man who had devoted his political life to the eradication of moral corruption, but who was utterly frustrated with the results so far. He claimed that there was a conspiracy against public liberty, that there were plotters among the members of the Convention, as well as among the members of the Committees of General Security and Public Safety. The remedy suggested by Robespierre was to "punish the traitors, purge the bureaux of the Committee of General Security, purge the Committee itself and subordinate it to the Committee of Public Safety, purge the Committee of Public Safety itself and create a unified government under the supreme authority of the Convention" (quoted in Hampson, p. 294).

The next day, the famous 9 Thermidor (27 July), Robespierre and the men close to him were outlawed by the Convention, and, following an abortive rescue mission by the Paris Commune and an unsuccessful attempt by Robespierre to kill himself, he was executed on 28 July.

A comparison of Meriwether Lewis and Maximilien Robespierre regarding the different forms of courage manifested in their lives indicates a possible explanation for Lewis' failure in his lack of a sense of moral responsibility and self-respect, both of which reveal an absence of the courage of conviction, while a similar possible explanation for Robespierre's failure could be found in his lack of the agency-related optimism inherent in the courage of creativity. From another point of view, it could be argued that Lewis failed because he had too much of the courage of creativity, while Robespierre failed because he had too much of the courage of conviction.

In Lewis' case, his optimism, which had contributed to his success as a expedition leader, seems to have turned into recklessness once he was given the opportunity and the liberty to do as he pleased. He was at his best when he had to perform in a well-defined context, which left room for him to develop his creative powers but at the same time confined those powers to the fulfilment of the specific requirements emanating from the assignment given to him by Jefferson. Once he was left free to define for himself what purposes and projects to accomplish, he seemed to be at a loss what to do, ending in a state of confusion, frustration, and despair.

With Robespierre it is the other way round. Being possessed by the courage of conviction, he came to view the world as a battleground, where justice was always threatened by corruption. His lack of optimism and trust in other people aggravated his sense of being positioned in a permanent state of emergency. His moral convictions made it possible for him to ignore his personal safety, but they also caused his relations with other people to be unnecessarily strained, as they admitted little compromise. Moral conviction in combination with a lack of optimism caused Robespierre to seek confrontation where he could not possibly win, antagonizing people who would have preferred to remain neutral, and, finally, brought about his downfall.

Irreconcilable Motivational Conflicts?

Now, it could be objected that it seems hard to reconcile the self-interested motivation behind the courage of creativity with the moral motivation that guides the courage of conviction. The will to achieve, which motivates the agent to develop in herself the courage of creativity, must, at least on certain occasions, conflict with the sense of moral responsibility, which motivates the agent to develop in herself the courage of conviction. Think, for instance, of Henry Stanley, famous for his persistent search for David Livingstone in the interior of Africa in 1871. Stanley clearly possessed the courage of creativity in the sense that he would not let himself be stopped by difficult terrain, long marches, tropical diseases, crocodiles, or whatever other kinds of obstacles he encountered as he set out to find Livingstone. Stanley's will to achieve was fuelled by his desire for fame. However, his will to achieve also made him reluctant to accept moral constraints, and this lack of moral consideration tainted his expedition with brutality. In the words of Adam Hochschild,

> Stanley was a harsh and brutal taskmaster. "The blacks give an immense amount of trouble; they are too ungrateful to suit my fancy," he wrote while on the journey…. He drove his men up hills and through swamps without letup. "When mud and wet sapped the physical energy of the lazily-inclined, a dog-whip became their backs, restoring them to a sound – sometimes to an extravagant

– activity." Only half a dozen years earlier Stanley had deserted from the U.S. Navy, but now he noted with satisfaction how "the incorrigible deserters ... were well flogged and chained." People in the villages that the expedition marched through may well have mistaken it for another slave caravan. (Hochschild, pp. 30–31.)

Now, it seems reasonable to assume that there will be cases in which the agent's will to achieve can be satisfied only at the expense of those legitimate interests of other people which her sense of moral responsibility enjoins her to respect. A successful businessman, for instance, may experience a conflict between his desire to make more money and his duty to serve his civic community in a just war. Likewise, a person may experience a conflict between defending a fellow worker's rights and the promotion of her own career.

To solve conflicts like these, we should remind ourselves that our will to achieve as well as our sense of moral responsibility both reflect different aspects of human agency. The will to achieve enables us to utilize our powers of agency for the sake of personal success, while the sense of moral responsibility, at least when guided by the *PGC*, makes us sensitive to the agency-related needs and rights of others.

As rational agents, we should accept restrictions on our will to achieve that derive from rights-claims that all agents must accept. For us to insist on a right to an unrestricted pursuit of our personal projects, while at the same time we demand of all other agents that they should respect our rights to freedom and well-being (and hence abstain from a right to an unrestrained pursuit of *their* personal projects), is to incur a logical inconsistency. Hence, we must accept that our duty to respect the generic rights of our recipients and to support the rights-protecting institutions of our civic community sets limits to our pursuit of our personal projects. In a case of conflict, the duty to participate in the defence of one's civic community in a just war overrides the right to enrich oneself. Likewise, in a case of conflict, the duty to defend an abused friend or a badly treated colleague overrides the right to promote one's career.

Now, there are also limits to what morality may require of us, but these limits do not derive from the will to achieve, but from the equality of rights upheld by the *PGC*. This equality of rights implies that the agent should assist her recipients in their efforts to maintain their rights, when she can do so *at no comparable cost to herself* (Gewirth, 1978, p. 218). Hence, the duty to help another person to protect her property is overridden if its fulfilment will cause the agent to lose her property. Likewise, the duty to rescue a person in mortal danger is overridden if the agent is bound to lose her own life in the process. (That the agent in this way may be relieved of her duty to *personally* assist her recipients does not, of course, imply that she is free to ignore other, less demanding, ways to help. She could, for instance, summon the police or some of her friends that are more fit to assist the persons in need of protection.)

However, there is reason to believe that the two forms of courage may function in a mutually reinforcing way when they are both present in an agent's character. An agent's sense of moral responsibility may, as it awakens her to the presence of important external goals in the world, also encourage her to make something of her personal talents in order to serve these external goals more efficiently. In the process, her capacity for creativity and personal achievement will benefit from her sense of moral responsibility. On the other hand, the capacity for creativity and personal achievement may generate a practical knowledge in the agent which will help her to apply her courage of conviction more realistically. A successful development of her personal talents and capabilities may then enhance her success as she strives to realize, for instance, some moral ideal. The people who rescued Jews from the Nazis during World War II knew well that moral conviction was not enough. They also needed the practical determination inherent in the courage of creativity, as well as the ability to focus on, and cope with, everyday practical matters:

> A core confidence, a strong sense of self, and a supportive situation had allowed bystanders to undertake the rescue. But once the decision to help had been reached and the rescue had begun, a different self – a *rescuer self* – emerged, to do what had to be done and to keep rescuers from becoming overwhelmed by new

responsibilities and pressures.... This new self, in the case of the rescuers, was built on strong moral foundations. It allowed them to do what was necessary – including plotting, stealing, lying, taking risks, enduring hardships, putting loved ones in jeopardy, and living in fear – all in the service of setting the world (and their place within it) on solid ground. (Fogelman, pp. 68–69.)

In Eva Fogelman's account above, the courage of creativity (determination in the face of adversities, resourcefulness under pressure) supports the courage of conviction (a sense of responsibility based on moral beliefs), while, simultaneously, creativity feeds on conviction. This is, I believe, a good illustration of a mutually supporting relationship between the two forms of courage.

CHAPTER 8

Heroism and Courage

As was indicated at the beginning of this study, courage has been regarded with some suspicion during the modern era, because of its believed affinity with the cult of heroism that lured so many young men to their destruction in World War I. In a time less prone to a rhetoric of courage and heroism, and more sceptical of Nietzschean overmen than, for instance, the late nineteenth century, the hero may indeed appear as suffering from certain flaws of character. Tzvetan Todorov, discussing the 1944 Polish partisan insurrection in Warsaw, points to a particular disregard for rational judgement in its leaders. Colonel Okulicki, the chief of operations for the Polish Home Army, adopted a heroic outlook from the beginning, and his "concern for what ought to be far outweighed his attention to what was" (Todorov, p. 6). One of the survivors of the uprising, Brigadier-General Tadeusz Pelczynski, interviewed thirty years after the event, took the same view: "We knew Poland was doomed, but we could not accept that verdict." Another survivor, General Tadeusz Bor-Komorovski, remembered that, on the eve of the insurrection, he just "discounted the possibility that it might fail". And, according to General Pelczynski, this attitude belongs to a military code of honour: "For a soldier … there is no order that cannot be carried out if he has the will to do so" (ibid.). This line of thinking manifested itself in the rather rigid outlook of Antoni Monter, the Home Army region commander for Warsaw, who, when told that a certain neighbourhood had fallen into German hands, replied: "I do not accept this information" (ibid.).

Todorov takes these observations regarding the leaders of the Warsaw uprising as a point of departure for some reflections concerning the hero:

> Heroes, then, prefer the ideal to the real – that much is certain. During the Warsaw Rising, the ideal went by several names. Clearly the rebels were fighting for the freedom of Warsaw (and, if possible, its survival); more often, however, they spoke in terms of a loftier ideal, that of "the nation." "We must fight," says Okulicki, "without regard for anything or anyone, and in our heart of hearts there can be only one thought – Poland" .... To claim that one's ideal is "the nation" is not enough, however, for the nation can be many things: a group of human beings – my family and friends or my compatriots, for instance – or a certain number of places and houses and roads. These interpretations Okulicki rejects: the uprising, he argues, must not be postponed "under the pretext of saving a few lives or a few houses" .... It is a question of saving not the people of Warsaw but the idea of Warsaw, not individual Poles or Polish territory but an abstraction called Poland. (Todorov, p. 7.)

Sometimes, Todorov notes, Poland is not an ideal sufficiently abstract and encompassing to suit the heroes of the rising, but is replaced with concepts such as "Western civilization" or even "humanity".

> The Russians are the forces of barbarism and Poland the last line of defense against them. Thus it becomes possible to sacrifice the lives of any number of people in the name of defending humanity. (Todorov, p. 8.)

The point is that it becomes increasingly difficult to claim that even the suicidal sacrifice of the whole Home Army is *not* justified, if a value such as "humanity" is at stake. When you are fighting for ideals of this moral magnitude and not just for the survival of human beings, quantitative arguments fail to persuade. How can you argue that humanity must not cost more than the lives of, let us say, ten thousand people? At this moment ends and means are easily conflated. Heroic consequentialism makes the will to be sacrificed a prime virtue. "We shall all be massacred ... but at least we will have fought", as one of the Warsaw insurgents commented (Todorov, p. 9). Given the purported moral significance of the end, any concern for the rights of individual human beings, or for prudence in general, will run the risk of appearing as a dishonourable mixture of selfishness and cowardice.

On the other hand, not all members of the Polish Home Army in Warsaw viewed the situation in this all-or-nothing manner. To at least one of them it was obvious that "[i]f all of us continue trying to die for Poland, one day soon there won't be any Poles left to live here" (Todorov, p. 10). This, however, would not be the heroic point of view, according to Todorov:

> To the hero, death has more value than life. Only through death – whether one's own or that of others – is it possible to attain the absolute: by dying for an ideal one proves that one holds it dearer than life itself. "Despair had driven them to aspire to the absolute," one witness says, "and at that level there was no solution but to die".... Measured against aspirations for the absolute, real life necessarily seems an unsatisfactory compromise. As another witness observes, "Heroes are not made to live" .... (Todorov, p. 10.)

Those who did not take the heroic view of the uprising were not advocating passivity. They did not argue in favour of surrender, but they thought it irresponsible to die just for the sake of proving themselves to be courageous. They met with little understanding from Colonel Okulicki, however, who called them cowards and violently denounced all who objected to the rising. Reflecting on the testimony of people who claimed they did not dare to question Okulicki's heroic position for fear of being called cowards or traitors, Todorov concludes that heroes are not immune to fear. It is rather that theirs is a fear of a particular kind, namely, "the fear of being afraid, and that feeling takes priority over all others and finally eclipses them" (Todorov, p. 11). This is an important observation, given our understanding of courage as the ability to confront one's fears. To the extent that Todorov's conclusion is correct, we may indeed question whether this kind of heroism deserves the name of courage.

Summing up his criticism of heroism, Todorov focuses on its categorical dualism, its all-or-nothing character:

> The hero's world – and perhaps herein lies his weakness – is one-dimensional; it is composed of pairs of opposites: us and them, friend and foe, courage and cowardice, hero and traitor, black and white. That outlook best befits situations in which the orientation is death, not life. In Warsaw of 1944, it was not simply the forces of good and evil that confronted each other but the Russians and the Germans, the Home Army and the People's Army, the government in exile and the civilian population. In circumstances this complex, reaching the best solution – in this instance, unfortunately, merely the lesser evil – requires a careful consideration of all sides rather than unswerving loyalty to an ideal. The values of life are not absolute values: life is diverse, and every situation is heterogeneous. Choices are made not out of concession or cowardly compromise but from a recognition of this multiplicity. (Todorov, p. 12.)

However, Todorov does not deny the desirability of heroic virtues when fighting a just war:

> From the minute it became clear that there was no other way to contain Hitler, going to war against him became the right choice; in circumstances like these, martial virtues and classical heroism seem to me entirely appropriate. I expect my military commander to be decisive, not hesitant or defeatist (I prefer Churchill to Chamberlain, de Gaulle to Daladier). I expect the soldier fighting beside me in the trenches to cover me to the end and not desert his post out of fear or indifference. Loyalty, courage, tenacity, and endurance are valued here; they are indispensable qualities. (Todorov, p. 53.)

Todorov insists, however, on the necessity of a particular context, namely, that of a just war, to justify heroism. Once the war is over, we should not look for leaders with heroic qualities:

> New situations demand new qualities: sending heroes into retirement once the war is over may be less an expression of ingratitude than a mark of lucidity. After the Second World War, Churchill and de Gaulle were no longer needed; left in power, they might have become dangerous. In normal times, democracy does quite

well without these "great men". As Brecht's Galileo says in a burst of true democratic spirit, "Woe to the country that needs heroes". (Todorov, pp. 53–54.)

The good hero, according to Todorov, is courageous but not reckless, aiming to ensure survival rather than death, and is making sacrifices for the sake of people rather than for the sake of abstract ideals. To clarify his idea of admirable heroism, Todorov gives us the story of Sacha Pechersky, the leader of the Sobibor rebellion in 1943. Pechersky, who before the war was a student of music, was captured by the Germans in 1941. He tried to escape, was recaptured, but managed to survive. In September 1943 he was sent to Sobibor. He almost immediately started to plan for revolt and escape. Pechersky established contact with other prisoners who had had war experience but who were still not broken physically and morally. He seems to have had no difficulties in finding friends and allies, not least because of his personal qualities: he is described as not only a man of dignity, but as good-humoured and attentive to other people. On 14 October the revolt began. Some Soviet POWs quietly killed isolated guards and took possession of their weapons. While Pechersky led an abortive attack on the camp arsenal, other prisoners cut a passage through the barbed wire to allow a mass escape. Out of four hundred prisoners who escaped, one hundred survived. Among them was Pechersky, who joined the resistance and lived to see the end of the war. Todorov concludes:

> Sacha Pechersky is the kind of hero one wants every hero in an extreme situation to be: decisive and effective but, at the same time, affectionate and temperate; he is not driven by ideology. Without him or someone like him, the Sobibor rebellion could not have happened. He took great risks to ensure the survival of at least a part of his community, but he saw to it that those risks were kept at a minimum. Forceful and courageous, he was also a man of good judgment; the classical hero he resembles most is Odysseus, leading his companions out of the cave of the Cyclops. And like Odysseus, Pechersky returned home and lived to a ripe old age, the one obstacle to his becoming a hero for popular consumption. (Todorov, p. 55.)

At this point we should sum up the relationship between various forms of heroism, as described by Todorov, and our present study of courage. One of the reasons why courage has got a bad name, at least in the eyes of some modern observers, is that it has been identified with the one-dimensional all-or-nothing heroism exemplified by Colonel Okulicki. This is the kind of courage to which Amélie Oksenberg Rorty's warning applies, that "[c]ourage is most dangerous when a person acts for the sake of being courageous, taking it to be an independent good, rather than one measured by its ends, bounded, checked and directed by other virtues" (Rorty, p. 153).

On the other hand, there is a form of heroism that appears attractive also to Todorov. He seems to base his distinction between good and bad heroism on how the heroic agent conceives of the purpose of her actions. While the "good" heroic agent regards her actions as instrumental to some worthy end, such as defeating the enemy, regaining one's freedom, or at least resisting being butchered by the enemy, "bad" heroic agents only care for the sacrificial aspects of the heroic act itself. Hence, Todorov's acceptance of the heroism of Churchill and de Gaulle, of the participants in the Warsaw ghetto uprising, and of Sacha Pechersky. The problem with Colonel Okulicki's heroism, on the other hand, is that it seems to have more to do with Okulicki's determination to make a noble sacrifice and so preserve his honour as well as the honour of the Home Army, rather than waging a war necessary to preserve Polish freedom. Accordingly, the "good" kind of heroism may more appropriately be called the *heroism of responsibility*, while the "bad" kind may be labelled the *heroism of honour*.

Continuing this line of reasoning, we may argue that the heroism of responsibility is simply the application of the courage of conviction to situations in which the agent willingly risks her own life. As is the case with the courage of conviction, the heroism of responsibility is motivated by a sense of moral responsibility. Unlike the courage of conviction, however, the heroism of responsibility requires not only that the agent is able to confront her fear of personal transience, but that there should actually be a danger to her life that she willingly confronts. Hence, the heroism of responsibility involves an objective component lacking in the courage of conviction. It does not suffice that the agent confronts a *fear* of personal transience, but this fear should be related to an actual (and not merely imagined) *danger* to her life. The heroism of honour, on the other hand, differs from the courage of conviction in that it is not motivated by any sense of moral responsibility on the agent's part, but rather by her desire for social recognition. The heroism of honour, however, shares with the heroism of responsibility the quality of being related to the agent's confronting an actual danger to her life. While the hero of responsibility emphasizes the significance of the end for which he is willing to risk his life, the hero of honour emphasizes the significance of being willing to die for that end.

For the hero of responsibility the important thing is that a certain significant end (the rescue of a friend in danger, the continued independence of his political community) is accomplished or at least brought closer to realization, whether or not his personal sacrifices are recognized. For the hero of honour, on the other hand, the important thing is that *he* has done what honour requires. And since "honour" is to a great extent a social phenomenon, that is, a question of what is *perceived* as honourable by one's peers, the hero of honour is likely to be very sensitive about how other people conceive of his actions and about their expectations regarding his future actions. Hence, it would be correct to say that the hero of honour is motivated, at least to some extent, by a desire for social recognition.

Now, although she does not fulfil the conditions of the courage of conviction (since she is not motivated by a sense of moral responsibility), the agent who manifests a heroism of honour is certainly not a coward. The heroism of honour involves confronting one's fear of dying as well as an actual danger to one's life. Hence, a hero of honour will not follow the coward's example and simply run away when he perceives danger. However, since he is motivated by a desire for social recognition and since he is to that extent also sensitive to how he is perceived by his peers, it could be plausibly argued that he will find it hard to confront the fear of *social* death. In fact, it could be argued that the fear of social death is, together with the positive desire for the recognition of others, a basic component of his motivation. As we noted above, Todorov diagnosed heroes like Colonel Okulicki as being driven by "the fear of being afraid". If we develop Todorov's analysis a bit further, we could argue that the heroes of honour are, at least to some extent, motivated by the fear of being *thought of* as afraid. And as this is an instance of the fear of social death, we have here another reason why the heroism of honour cannot qualify as an extension of the courage of conviction.

The heroism of responsibility, on the other hand, shares with the courage of conviction the quality of being motivated by the agent's sense of moral responsibility. This entails that the hero of responsibility carefully adjusts his actions so that they are consistent with the values that he wants to uphold. But unlike the hero of honour, the hero of responsibility does not fear for what other people might think of his action, and is to that extent immune to the fear of social death. He may risk his life, if necessary, for the sake of his nation, his religious beliefs, the rights of his fellow citizens, or whatever moral goal is important to him, but he will not risk his life just for the sake of proving himself worthy of the esteem of other members of his community. In fact, the hero of responsibility might act contrary to the prevailing code of honour in his community, should that code conflict with what he believes to be morally right. Hence he would share Sidgwick's reluctance to identify morality with honour:

> [I]n the ordinary thought of unreflective persons the duties imposed by social opinion are often undistinguished from moral duties: and indeed this indistinctness is almost inherent in the common meaning of many terms. For instance, if we say that a man has been 'dishonoured' by a cowardly act, it is not quite clear whether we mean that he has incurred contempt, or that he has deserved it, or both: as becomes evident when we take a case in which the Code of Honour comes into conflict with Morality. If (*e.g.*) a man were to incur social ostracism anywhere for refusing a duel on religious grounds, some would say that he was 'dishonoured,' though he had acted rightly, others that there could be no real dishonour in a virtuous act. (Sidgwick, pp. 30–31.)

To sum up, unlike the courage of conviction, heroism is not only about being able to confront one's fear of personal transience, but also about being able to confront an actual danger to one's life and to willingly risk one's life in that confrontation. There are two kinds of heroism, the heroism of responsibility and the heroism of honour. The heroism of responsibility is an extension of the courage of conviction, as all heroes of responsibility by definition also possess the courage of conviction; the reverse relationship does not hold, however. The heroism of honour, on the other hand, is inconsistent with the courage of conviction, as it is, at least to some extent, motivated by the agent's fear of social death; this, however, does not imply that heroes of honour are cowards.

Now, for a *morally justified* heroism of responsibility it is not sufficient that the end of the heroic action, e.g., the freedom of a civic community, is morally justified. The agent of a morally justified heroism must also choose her means to that end in a way that expresses her sense of moral responsibility for the rights of her recipients, and this requirement sets limits to the risks she can ask her recipients to take. For instance, she cannot require of them that they should join a battle against overwhelming odds, when it is possible both to avoid that battle and to accomplish one's goals by other means. And even if freedom may be temporarily lost in a conflict with a more powerful aggressor, this may have to be accepted, if the only likely alternative is a wholesale massacre of members of one's political community, and if there is hope of regaining freedom, at least in a long-term perspective. To the extent that such a hope is realistic, life must be chosen over freedom, "but only with the fullest resolve to fight for freedom at the earliest available opportunity" (Gewirth, 1978, p. 349). (Things will look different, however, if the aggressor's intention is to permanently enslave one's political community, or even to exterminate its members. In cases of this extremity, there will indeed be nothing lost in fighting as hard as one can, even if the only advantage will be that of dying standing on one's feet, arms in hand, rather than on one's knees with one's hands tied behind one's back.)

Now, although the person who is, in Todorov's words, "driven by ideology" may often be a particularly ruthless character (as, for instance, in the case of dedicated SS officers or Soviet communist party commissars), we should not conclude that the heroes we approve of could do without "ideology". The heroism of responsibility as well as the courage of conviction require a view of the world such as that there are at least some things that are more important than the agent's personal well-being. We may disapprove of a particular hero's ideology, but we should not construe our view of the difference between bad and good heroes as the difference between those who do and those who do not have their courage infused with moral ideals. Rather, it is the *contents* of these moral ideals and the *means* whereby they are realized that should determine our assessment of heroes and heroic actions.

Todorov's criticism of abstract idealism in heroes, as well as our discussion of the heroism of honour, may be amplified in an interesting way by the analysis of the concept of constitutional cowardice, originally suggested by the philosopher and World War II soldier J. Glenn Gray. In Douglas Walton's words, the constitutional coward, when in battle, "simply cannot manage to endure personal danger with composure and feels that every bullet is intended for him" (Walton, p. 103). So far, this observation of the paralysing effect of pessimism underlines the importance of adding the positive planning of the courage of creativity to the courage of conviction, noted above in connection with the cases of Lewis and Robespierre. But what is really interesting here is Gray's explanation for constitutional cowardice, as recounted by Walton, in terms of the coward's dissociation from others:

> Gray ... observed that the constitutional coward tends to be constantly troubled by his own imagination – he sees potential danger everywhere and is constantly on the move to find a safer spot. He gives an example of a man in his unit who was constantly worried about his safety, even sleeping in a ravine full of red ants one night after a bombing instead of staying in a chalet with the rest of the platoon.
>
> In answer to the query of what makes the constitutional coward so different from the average soldier, Gray offers the hypothesis that this type of individual lacks the sense of union with his comrades

> that the other men share. In a way, Gray's explanation suggests that the behavior of the constitutional coward is consistent with the inner logic of his beliefs. It is an observation of Gray's that most soldiers have a joy in sacrifice and will often give up their lives easily for the necessity of the group in combat. However, the constitutional coward is unable to understand this altruistic behavior. For him, the value of the group does not outweigh the value of his own life. This individual, as Gray puts it ..., has one answer to arguments concerning his duty or respect toward his friends: "What do they matter if I am no longer alive to know about them?"... The failure here, according to Gray, is a deficiency of love, an inability to participate in the lives of others. According to him, the spectacle of the death of this sort of coward is a most unpleasant scene. (Walton, pp. 103–104.)

Now, this "deficiency of love" that Gray finds in the constitutional coward may be very relevant to the criticism of the heroism of honour. Agents who are committed to the heroism of honour, and who are willing to sacrifice their own lives as well as the lives of those under their command for the sake of honour and social recognition, are certainly not cowards. They do not try to escape death, but rather seek it out. But in this they may also show themselves as just as deficient in love of their fellow men as the constitutional coward, as they force them to join in their sacrificial project. Just like the constitutional coward, they are unable to participate in the lives and concerns of ordinary human beings, being too preoccupied with proving themselves to history as true heroes. And this may well constitute a justified moral criticism on the lines suggested by Todorov.

The agent committed to the heroism of honour, courting death as a pathway to fame and glory, fails to recognize that to most human beings their lives are precious, and that although most of us may accept that there are causes worth fighting and, if necessary, dying for, we do not make these decisions with a light heart. Not just any cause is worth dying for, and even if the cause is sufficiently worthy (e.g., the freedom of our civic community), we are not prepared to sacrifice our lives for its sake unless this is really necessary. That is, it is not enough to die for a good cause, but we want to be sure that our sacrifice makes a practical difference. Hence, if we can achieve our worthy end *without* sacrificing our lives, or if it is *impossible* to achieve that end whether we sacrifice our lives or not, then we have no good reason to sacrifice our lives, whatever the value of the end in question. (The exception would be those tragic cases in which the future to be expected is so grim that it is better to die fighting than to surrender. But then the reason for choosing to die fighting is not that death on the battlefield is particularly honourable, but rather that surrendering only brings with it the prospect of being butchered or enslaved by the merciless conquerors.) The agent committed to the heroism of honour is likely to fail to understand these aspects. She rejects the idea that a "glorious" cause may be assessed in terms of its consequences for individual human beings. And she rejects the idea that means such as passive resistance or civil disobedience sometimes may be preferred to open military confrontation with a militarily superior enemy. This kind of agent prefers open battle and a "honourable" death to the patient, long-term subversive work that may keep resistance alive without incurring the destructive costs of warfare. And in this she seems to share the constitutional coward's deficiency of love for her fellow comrades in arms.

The distinction between a desirable form of courage and a morally dubious heroism of honour seems to be recognized also among combat soldiers themselves. Sanimir Resic, in his study of American soldiers in Vietnam, gives a picture of how martial virtues were conceived by the GIs:

> The conception of *courage* tended to be expressed as uncomplaining endurance, perseverance and self-sacrificial acts in saving comrades' lives. Such behavior and deeds of bravery never lost their value and appreciation among the combat soldiers. Soldiers who performed acts of bravado on the other hand, the so-called Heroes, were seen as a liability. Also, the wish to prove one's manhood in combat decreased in general as a result of combat experience. (Resic, p. 244.)

The American Civil War Experience

Sometimes there is reason to believe that certain actions which we are disposed to think of as instances of the heroism of responsibility in fact may prove to be instances of the heroism of honour, motivated at least to some extent by the agent's fear of social death, and to that extent inconsistent with the requirements of the courage of conviction.

The 1861–65 American Civil War exemplifies a conflict in which soldiers on both sides were highly motivated by moral convictions and in which we find many examples of the heroism of responsibility, but also some instances of the heroism of honour. In general, moral motivation seems to have been a major factor in explaining the soldiers' endurance in an extremely devastating conflict. As historian James M. McPherson points out:

> Duty and honor were indeed powerful motivating forces. They had to be, for some other traditional reasons that have caused men to fight in organized armies had little relevance in the Civil War. Religious fanaticism and ethnic hatreds played almost no role. Discipline was notoriously lax in Civil War volunteer regiments. Training was minimal by modern standards. The coercive power of the state was flaccid. Subordination and unquestioning obedience to orders were alien to this most democratic and individualistic of nineteenth-century societies. (McPherson, pp. 5–6.)

The moral motivation of Civil War soldiers could not deceive them about the horrors of battlefields and forced marches. But it gave them a perspective on these horrors that turned them into meaningful and justified sacrifices. As one Pennsylvania officer wrote to his wife:

> [S]ick as I am of this war and bloodshed [and] as much oh how much I want to be home with my dear wife and children … every day I have a more religious feeling, that this war is a crusade for the good of mankind.… I [cannot] bear to think of what my children would be if we were to permit this hell-begotten conspiracy to destroy this country. (McPherson, p. 13.)

Fiancées, wives, and parents did not always share the patriotic commitment of the young soldiers, which sometimes caused the latter to reproach their loved ones back home. A recruit in the 11th Michigan wrote to his fiancée who had asked him not to enlist (absence of punctuation and capitalization as in the original):

> No Jenny ... while your happiness is as dear to me as life duty prompts me to go my country first home and friends next Jenny what would friends be to me if I had no country? (McPherson, p. 23.)

And a soldier in the 18th Georgia, writing to his wife, who had told him that his two daughters were pleading for him to come home, also concluded in favour of what he saw as his moral responsibility as a Southerner (spelling as in the original):

> I came to the war because I felt it to be my duty ... I am not going to run away if I never come home I had rather di without seeing them than for peple to tell them after I am dead that their father was a deserter.... It [is] every Southern mans duty to fight against abolition misrule and preserve his Liberty untarnished which was won by our fore Fathers.... I never yet regreted the step I have taken. (McPherson, p. 138.)

Likewise, an Irish-born carpenter, who had joined the 28th Massachusetts, rebuked both his wife and his father-in-law back in Ireland for questioning his decision to fight for Lincoln:

> This is my country as much as the man who was born on the soil ... I have as much interest in the maintenance of ... the integrity of the nation as any other man.... This is the first test of a modern free government in the act of sustaining itself against internal enemys ... if it fail all tyrants will succeed the old cry will be sent forth from the aristocrats of europe that such is the common lot of all republics. (McPherson, p. 113.)

The statements quoted above indicate a sense of moral responsibility, motivating the soldiers not only to confront their fear of personal transience, but also to perform actions of the kind associated with the heroism of responsibility:

> Sacrifice on the "alter" (a frequent misspelling) of one's country was a typical phrase in soldier letters. So were the words written by a Missouri Confederate soldier to his wife in 1862 that she should take comfort in "knowing that if I am killed that I die fighting for my Country and my rights." Two months later she learned that this grim foreboding had come true. A lieutenant in the 47th Alabama wrote his wife in 1862: "I confess that I gave you up with reluctance. Yet I love my country [and] … intend to discharge my duty to my country and to my God." He too never returned to his wife and two children he missed so much. (McPherson, p. 95.)

James McPherson, who has studied the letters and diaries of more than a thousand Union and Confederate soldiers and officers, found that 66 per cent of the Confederate soldiers explicitly referred to patriotic motivation at one time or another after enlisting; the corresponding figure for Union soldiers is 68 per cent. Of McPherson's sample 21 per cent were killed or mortally wounded in action (McPherson, pp. 100–101, 103). Hence, he concludes, we should take their professed patriotism seriously:

> They were not posturing for public show. They were not looking back from years later through a haze of memory and myth about the Civil War. They were writing during the immediacy of their experiences to explain and justify their beliefs to family members and friends who shared – or in some cases questioned – those beliefs. And how smugly can we sneer at their expressions of a willingness to die for those beliefs when we know that they did precisely that? (McPherson, p. 100.)

To what extent did these moral convictions actually enhance combat courage? It is of course a difficult question to answer, but judging from the surviving testimonies of the officers and soldiers who were on the battle scenes, the commitment to a just cause seems to have played an important role in many cases. "The Only thing that bears me up ... in the hour of Battles is the Consciousness ... that I am in discharge of a duty that all good sitizens owe their country" one captain of the 37th North Carolina wrote. "It is the caus that makes a man fight" wrote a sergeant in the 59th Illinois after the battle of Pea Ridge (McPherson, p. 115; spelling as in the original). When Union commander Nathaniel Banks called for volunteers to form a special unit of shock troops to lead assaults, one of them gave his reasons for volunteering: "I thought of the mighty interests at stake ... and I concluded that the great results which it promised were worth the sacrifice" (McPherson, p. 115). And historian James McPherson concludes that "[t]he ideological commitment of so many of those volunteers of 1861 and 1862 was one reason for the high casualty rates of Civil War armies" (p. 116).

However, moral commitment was not always sufficient to sustain combat courage in the face of defeat. A soldier in the 23rd Massachusetts, which was badly thrashed at Drewry's Bluff and Cold Harbor, confessed in the summer of 1864 that "in view of the fate of my regiment I must admit that my patriotism is somewhat shaken.... We are all very low spirited.... *All looks dark*.... It is time we should acknowledge that the northern army can never subdue the South" (McPherson, p. 161). But in early 1865 it was Confederate soldiers who foresaw defeat. A soldier in the 58th Virginia wrote to his sister that "many have come to the belief that we will never whip the Yankees and it is only a question of time to bring us under.... Many are anxious for the war to stop and they don't care how [just] so they get out of the Army" (McPherson, p. 162).

Lack of sleep, hunger, physical and mental exhaustion also broke many of the Civil War soldiers. James McPherson tells the story of the colonel of the élite 20th Massachusetts who broke down after the battle of Antietam:

> The next morning he rode away from camp without telling anyone and was later found "without a cent in his pocket, without anything to eat or drink, without having changed his clothes for 4 weeks, during all which time he had this horrible diarrhea.... He was just like a little child wandering away from home." (McPherson, p. 165).

Still, it seems that the perception of duty prevailed among many of the soldiers who fought to the end of the war. According to McPherson, "the values of duty and honor remained a crucial component of their sustaining motivation to the end" (p. 168). He cites a soldier in the 89th Illinois, writing to his mother who had urged him to get a medical discharge after he was wounded at Pickett's Mills in May 1864. (She had already lost one son killed in action.) The soldier, however, insisted on returning to the army:

> Because I have done my Duty for the last 23 months ... that is no reason why I should not return to the regiment and do my Duty again. (McPherson, p. 169.)

Now, the decision to stay on and continue fighting, even in the face of dismal prospects, was not only an indication of the individual soldier's moral conviction regarding the cause he was fighting for, but also an effect of group pressure. While a sense of moral responsibility related to membership in the wider community, i.e., the American nation, one's state, or the Union, played an important part in motivating soldiers to enlist, it seems as if it was their membership in the smaller community of the combat unit which generated in them a sense of moral responsibility that actually made them fight and endure the hardships of battle.

> Bonded by the common danger they face in battle, this primary group becomes a true band of brothers whose mutual dependence and mutual support create the cohesion necessary to function as a fighting unit. The survival of each member of the group depends on the others doing their jobs; the survival of the group depends on the steadiness of each individual. It is the primary group that enforces peer pressure against cowardice. If any member of the group "plays off" or succumbs to "cannon fever" during combat, he not only dangers his own and the others' survival but he also courts their contempt and ostracism; he loses self-respect as a man and may be exiled by the group. For many soldiers this could be quite literally a fate worse than death; it was a powerful incentive for fight rather than flight. (McPherson, pp. 85–86.)

However, group pressure may contribute not only to the ability of soldiers to endure the horrors of war, but it may also generate a heroism of honour, as soldiers become motivated to risk their lives just for the sake of not being thought of as cowards. Think of these cases, related by McPherson:

> Soldiers who went into action despite a real illness sometimes paid a steep price. A private in the 62nd Pennsylvania remained with his regiment despite the surgeon's orders to the contrary, for "if I had of Staid behind I would have been called a coward." He later regretted this decision, for he became seriously ill and did not recover for weeks just because "my foolish Pride kept me in the ranks." A corporal in the 1st Minnesota fought at First Bull Run despite sickness and afterward lost sixty pounds and almost died during three months in an army hospital. The 2nd Massachusetts was one of the war's elite regiments, with many of its officers from Boston's Brahmin class. One of them, Robert Gould Shaw, reported that four of his fellow officers refused to stay out of the battle of Cedar Mountain even though they were "quite ill." "It was splendid," Shaw wrote his mother, "to see those sick fellows walk straight up into the shower of bullets, as if it were so much rain." For that splendor three of the four paid with their lives. (McPherson, p. 79.)

Now, there is nothing splendid about sick men willingly sacrificing their lives just for the sake of preserving their honour. It is simply a waste of human lives. And it is cases like the one observed by Shaw that have given heroism, and by association, also courage, a bad name. But to choose to put one's life at risk just out of a fear of what others might think if one did not, is not courage at all, as it reflects a fear of social death. Good heroism, that is, a heroism of responsibility that is also consistent with the requirements of the *PGC*, means that the agent should make assessments of *moral necessity* before any person's life is put at risk (including the life of the agent herself). An agent's life, being her most important good of agency, should not be jeopardized, not even by herself, just for the sake of preserving a less important good, such as high social status.

A person may still function as an agent without being "splendid" in the sense indicated above, that is, being highly esteemed by her peers, but without life she cannot act at all. Hence, according to the criterion of degrees of needfulness for action, since life is needed for action more than high social status is, the former should never be sacrificed for the sake of the latter.

Moreover, a person should never be required to risk her life in battle unless this is necessary for the defence of the rights-protecting institutions of the civic community of which she is a member, and without which neither she nor other members of that community will enjoy the freedom and well-being generally necessary to all successful agency. Since the civic community is a morally necessary form of community, it is also a moral duty for each and every one of its members to participate in its defence whenever this is needed. However, the duty in question is to contribute to the defence of the civic community rather than risking one's life. Of course, when participating in a war to defend one's civic community, it would be difficult not to risk one's life, at least in cases of direct confrontation with the enemy. Still, what is morally required is not heroic bravado, but as efficient a contribution as possible to the end of protecting one's civic community. Risking one's life may be a predictable side-effect of one's contribution to the defence of one's civic community, but this does not mean that it is a desired side-effect, still less that it is a desired end in its own right.

Heroism and Ordinary Virtues

Now, after having discussed at some length martial applications of the heroism of responsibility, we should remind ourselves that this kind of heroism does not only apply to soldiers, but to any individual who willingly risks her life out of a sense of moral responsibility, the object of which may be another individual's survival and dignity, or some other end that the agent finds morally important. Todorov's discussion of the "ordinary virtues" of dignity and caring contains some good examples of what we have called the heroism of responsibility.

Todorov relates the case of Marek Edelman, a survivor of the

Warsaw ghetto rising in 1943, and his description of how he came to be a resistance fighter. Edelman witnessed how two German officers hoisted an old Jewish man up onto a barrel and, laughing, cut off his beard with a huge pair of tailor's scissors. "At that moment," Edelman said, "I realized that the most important thing was never letting myself be pushed onto the top of that barrel. Never, by anybody" (Todorov, p. 15). Even if resistance meant death, it would still be preferable to die fighting, rather than just be butchered.

> What Edelman understood is, first that there is no qualitative difference between great and small humiliations and, second, that one can always express one's will, choose one's actions – and refuse to follow orders. The uprising may have been nothing more than a way for us to choose our death, he says. But the difference between choosing death and submitting to it is enormous; it is this difference that separates human beings from animals. In choosing one's death, one performs an act of will and thereby affirms one's membership in the human race.... *Dignity:* this, then is the first ordinary virtue, and it simply means the capacity of the individual to remain a subject with a will; that fact, by itself, is enough to ensure membership in the human race. (Todorov, pp. 15–16.)

As for the other ordinary virtue, that of caring, Todorov relates a story, told by Marek Edelman, about a young girl called Pola Lifszyc, whose mother had been picked up by the Germans for further transportation to Treblinka:

> "She went to her house and ... saw that her mother wasn't there," Edelman says. "Her mother was already in a column marching toward the *Umschlagplatz.* Pola ran after the column alone, from Leszno Street to Stawki Street. Her fiancé gave her a lift in his *riksa* so that she could catch up – and she made it. At the last minute, she managed to merge into the crowd so as to be able to get on the train with her mother" .... (The train, of course, was one of those whose passengers never returned to their point of departure.) (Todorov, p. 17.)

But in what way are Edelman's decision to defend his dignity and Pola Lifszyc's decision to join her mother on her journey to death in Treblinka different from that of Colonel Okulicki to rise against the Germans? After all, is not the Colonel defending his dignity when he refuses to retreat? Is he not caring about Polish morale when he orders his men to fight against all odds?

For Todorov the difference between the heroism of Colonel Okulicki and the ordinary virtues concerns how the agent views life and death, and the purpose of her sacrifice. A hero like Colonel Okulicki, according to Todorov, seeks death, while the person protecting her dignity has no desire to die, but is prepared to do so, should there be no other way out:

> For the hero, death eventually becomes a value and a goal, because it embodies the absolute better than life does. From the standpoint of the ordinary virtues, however, death is a means, not an end: it is the ultimate recourse of the individual who seeks to affirm his dignity. (Todorov, p. 16.)

Hence, Todorov considers the Warsaw ghetto uprisning of 1943 a "sane reaction" in a way the Warsaw uprising of 1944 was not. The ghetto was doomed anyway, and even if the uprising may not have saved any lives "the fact that it happened at all may well have helped others to live by showing them the possibility of active resistance". As for the Warsaw uprising of 1944, "this revolt was not really inevitable; rather, it resulted from a calculation that proved erroneous, in a situation that offered other possibilities" (pp. 25–26).

What Todorov captures here, however, is not the distinction between heroism and non-heroism, but that between the heroism of honour and the heroism of responsibility. It is the difference between sacrifices made for the sake of the agent's commitment to a code of honour (Colonel Okulicki's determination to fight, regardless of the other options at hand), and those made out of a sense of moral responsibility (the determination of the ghetto insurgents to fight in defence of their dignity, knowing that the people in the ghetto were doomed anyway).

As for 'caring', Todorov wants to restrict the application of this concept to cases in which the agent contributes to the welfare of individuals. Hence, the abstract ideals of Colonel Okulicki do not qualify him as a caring person, since

> acts of ordinary virtue are undertaken not in behalf of humanity or the nation but always for the sake of an individual human being. (Todorov, p. 17.)

Here I disagree with Todorov, however. It is not the fact that Okulicki wants to serve his nation rather than individual human beings that makes his brand of heroism objectionable, but rather the fact that he seems to think of the heroic sacrifice as necessitated by an aristocratic and military concept of honour, rather than by the plight of his nation. Likewise, Todorov argues that the sacrifice of Father Maximilian Kolbe would not qualify as an instance of caring. Kolbe volunteered in Auschwitz to die in the place of a man singled out for death by starvation. Kolbe knew that the man in question had a wife and children, but, Todorov assumes, he probably "died less for Franciszek Gajowniczek ... than to fulfill his Christian duty" (p. 55). Hence, Kolbe in fact sacrificed himself for the sake of an ideal rather than for the sake of a particular individual human being, which excludes his act from being an instance of caring. However, regardless of whether it was his Christian faith or his compassion for the individual Franciszek Gajowniczek that motivated Kolbe, we will have no difficulty in recognizing it as an instance of the heroism of responsibility, since Kolbe willingly gives up his life out of a sense of moral responsibility.

Now, caring, as an ordinary virtue, may in extreme circumstances imply killing the people one cares for. Todorov cites Edelman, who tells us about a doctor who poisoned the children in the hospital where she worked, before the SS came to take them away to the gas chamber. In so doing she sacrificed her own cyanide, a poison that doctors and nurses used to save for their closest relatives (p. 19).

However, when death is avoidable, caring means helping one's neighbour to survive rather than helping her to die. In the concentration camps many people survived only because of the assistance they received from fellow inmates. Sharing food and rags of clothes, hiding someone who is called out for selection (for the gas chamber), saving someone from being raped, refusing to denounce a fellow prisoner who has stolen and instead accepting punishment for the theft – acts like these are frequently mentioned by surviving prisoners of both German concentration camps and Soviet Gulag camps (Todorov, pp. 72–73.) Caring about others has its own rewards in extreme circumstances like these, as Todorov points out, since it is likely to take the agent's mind off her own suffering and despair (pp. 88–89). Hence, caring may fortify the agent against that particular fear which we have called the fear of meaninglessness, and may so constitute an essential contribution to the development of the courage of conviction. In this way, acts of caring in extreme circumstances may both express and reinforce the agent's courage, even to the extent of enabling her to perform actions of the kind associated with the heroism of responsibility. Moreover, caring may also contribute to the maintenance of dignity, since the recipient of the caring act is "recognized as a human being who is capable of becoming not only the instrument of an action but also its end" (Todorov, p. 87). Likewise, the caring agent is in her action reminded of herself as a moral subject, which may have a beneficial impact on her self-respect and will to survive:

> Perhaps by caring about others, one experiences a recovery of one's own dignity and self-respect because one is doing something recognized as morally laudable, and that feeling of dignity, in itself, strengthens one's ability to stay alive. (Todorov, p. 88.)

The virtues of dignity and caring may conflict, however, in that the agent's concern to maintain the dignity of herself and her group may cause her to ignore the negative impacts of that concern on the well-being of the members of the group in question. Todorov gives us the example of Alma Rose, the conductor of the women's orchestra at Auschwitz, for whom musical perfection took precedence over all humanitarian consideration. Rose claimed that "[d]ying is unimportant; what is important, truly important, is to play music". Todorov continues:

> Her arrival in Auschwitz allowed her to devote herself to music, and the shortcomings of her musicians were simply obstacles to be overcome.... Rose shouted and slapped and rationalized. "Here or elsewhere," she said, "whatever one does should be done well, if only out of self-respect".... Once again, we see how artistic and intellectual activity can give rise to feelings of dignity – pride in the knowledge of a job well done – while ignoring the interests of the individuals involved. (Todorov, p. 105.)

Acts of caring, although they express a moral position of an agent, are often done without explicitly invoking moral principles. That is, moral principles do not appear in the agent's subjectively experienced motives for her actions. They are done simply because the agent cares about her recipients, conceiving of their well-being as an object of her responsibility. The agent may act from the emotion of sympathy rather than from an adherence to a particular moral theory or principle. Although this emotion by itself implies moral convictions and moral beliefs about what is right and wrong to do, the agent may, when confronted with moral language, fail to recognize its application to her actions. Philip Hallie describes the reaction of Magda Trocmé, who during World War II helped to rescue Jewish children from the Nazis in occupied France, when he expressed his admiration for her work:

> That first afternoon, overwhelmed by these thoughts, I found myself whispering half to myself and half to Magda Trocmé words that came from the same deep levels of my being from which tears had sprung: "But you are good people, good."
> To anger an Italian is usually not hard to do ..., but I was still surprised and a little daunted at Magda Trocmé's sudden and vehement reaction to my words. "What did you say? *What?* 'Good'? *Good?*"
> I muttered something like, "Yes, I mean – "
> She interrupted herself and me in a quiet, sympathetic voice: "I'm sorry, but you see, you have not understood what I have been saying. We have been talking about saving the children. We did not do what we did for goodness' sake. We did it for the children.

Don't use words like 'good' with me. They are foolish words." (Hallie, p. 31.)

Certain daring aspects of acts of caring, like the ones performed by rescuers of Jews during World War II, also serve as a further substantiation of the distinction between the heroism of honour and the heroism of responsibility. For, as Eva Fogelman has made very clear, the heroism of these rescuers often meant that they acted *against* the prevailing views of their communities. Hence, their actions were not guided by a desire for social recognition, as would have been the case if they had been heroes of honour, but rather by a sense of moral responsibility that made them defy the normative expectations of their peers.

> When bystanders transformed themselves into rescuers, they put concern for their own survival in the background and took responsibility for the well-being of others. They became outlaws in a Nazi no-man's-land. Their ideas of right and wrong were out of fashion. This was new for them, since before the war they had been very much part of their communities. Most rescuers were not loners or people who felt alienated from society. But the secret of rescue effectively isolated them from everyone else. Neighbors viewed people who harbored Jews as selfish and dangerous because they risked their lives and the lives of those around them. (Fogelman, pp. 67–68.)

Hence, instead of being able to rely on the esteem and solidarity of their fellow community members, the rescuers of Jews had to guard themselves constantly against betrayal by Nazi collaborators. "A careless word, a forgotten detail, or one wrong move could lead to death" (Fogelman, p. 68). And even after the war, many rescuers had to keep their heroic acts to themselves for fear of anti-Semitic retaliation:

> Rescuers in Eastern Europe, the Ukraine, Poland, and Russia, who lived among Jew-hating neighbors, extracted promises from their charges not to reveal their rescue role, and then, with the utmost

caution, they helped their charges scurry away.... For Jews and their rescuers, postwar Poland was a hostile environment. Most Jews, and some of their saviors, felt they had no choice but to emigrate. In fact, the great majority of rescuers who left Europe did so because they continued to feel that their lives were in danger because they had saved Jews.... Vigilance, secrecy, cunning, and role-playing were still needed for self-protection. Polish partisans and bandits roamed the countryside looking for Jews and "Jew-lovers" to kill. (Fogelman, pp. 274–275.)

The German industrialist Oskar Schindler, who during the war sheltered 1,200 Jews from deportation to death camps by recruiting them as workers and then insisting to the Nazi authorities that they were essential to the German war effort, found that he was not universally admired for what he had done.

In Tel Aviv, he was hailed on the streets as a hero. In Frankfurt, where he lived, he was jeered at and pelted with stones. In 1963, he punched a factory worker who called him a "Jew-kisser," and the man lodged a charge of assault. The local judge lectured Schindler and then ordered him to pay damages. (Fogelman, p. 291.)

We may safely conclude that the rescuers of Jews during World War II were heroes of responsibility, acting from a sense of moral duty that often made them go against the opinion prevailing in their communities. They were definitely not heroes of honour, seeking the social recognition of their peers.

One morally significant aspect of these rescuing activities is that they often involve a sensitive conflict of duties on the rescuing agent's part, between her commitment to the safety of her family and her commitment to the safety of those innocent strangers whom she is trying to protect from being murdered. Sometimes children were actively involved in rescuing operations, and even when they were not, they were nevertheless compromised by their parents' activities and likely to share their fate should the Germans find out what they were up to.

> To this day, Johtje Vos is horrified by what she did. It was at a time when a member of their rescue network had been arrested. Everyone's life was in danger. The Voses sat down with their fugitives to decide what to do. In preparation for a move to another hiding place, Johtje Vos had retrieved their real papers. Without warning, the Germans arrived. Aart Vos and the Jews ran for the tunnel. With the children upstairs napping, Johtje Vos realized she could not leave. She scooped up the papers and, desperate for a place to hide them, stuffed them into the pocket of the sweater her son was wearing. "Quietly try to get out of here and disappear with the papers," she ordered him. He did as he was told. As it happened, no one was arrested, but it was the narrowest of escapes. Afterward, Johtje Vos was appalled that she risked her son's life that way. (Fogelman, pp. 81–82.)

Some of the rescuers' children expressed mixed feelings about their parents' choice to endanger their families for the sake of saving strangers. Esther Warmerdam recalls her childhood home being searched by German soldiers for hidden Jews, one of them putting a gun to her father's head. Her mother rushed to his assistance, telling the Germans that her husband was a deafmute:

> Suddenly we heard a shot and we thought it was over. A few moments later, he came into the house smiling. He told us how proud he was that we kept our mouths shut…. If only he knew how I had felt inside. I was ready to run outside and tell them…. Enough was enough. Tears were not there anymore, only anger. Anger at my parents and the whole stinking world. We had not asked for this. (Quoted in Fogelman, p. 224.)

Eva Fogelman explains the difficulties these children of rescuers must have had in fully sympathizing with their parents' choice:

> [R]escue took over every aspect of family life. All other concerns were pushed aside…. No matter what troubles or problems a child might have, they appeared insignificant compared with those that faced Jews. Guilt, shame, and anger vied with the child's feelings

of love and pride. They empathized with the plight of the Jews while at the same time they resented them. They were angry at their parents for undertaking a humanitarian role in which they were forced to take part, while admiring them for their altruism. Above all, they could not help asking the question that haunted Esther Warmerdam decades later: "Why were my parents doing this to me?" They chose to put their children's lives in danger. Why?... A startling one-quarter of all those rescuers I interviewed said they risked the lives of their children to save others. Parents, who sometimes used children as young as five years old as couriers or decoys, felt guilty that they risked their children's lives to save the lives of comparative strangers. (Fogelman, p. 225.)

Now, we must ask ourselves whether or not it could be a morally justified heroism of responsibility to risk one's children's lives for the sake of rescuing the lives of persecuted strangers. It could be argued that, while the parents were free to risk their own lives to rescue Jews, they had no right to risk their children's lives, at least not in those cases in which the children were too young to make a choice of their own (for instance, to stay out of trouble by leaving home). Just as we cannot morally require of a person who is unable to swim that she should jump into the ocean to save a drowning man, we should not require children who are unable to take care of themselves to participate in rescue operations which may cost them their lives. The fact that the children in question depend on us for their well-being does not reduce them to a resource for us to employ as we see fit. On the contrary, it should make us extremely careful that nothing bad happens to them while they are in our custody. And if we believe that child labour is wrong, then we should also reject the idea of children rescuers.

This is indeed a plausible and powerful argument for the conclusion that parents who are freely undertaking some dangerous project should not enlist their children in that project. And it seems that at least some of the rescuers who risked their children's lives also recognized the force of this argument, as they later admitted to feelings of guilt for what they had made their children go through.

On the other hand, it could be argued that the risk to the children's lives in the rescue operations under discussion did not come from their parents, but from German soldiers, Nazi collaborators, and other agents of evil. Should we hold the parents responsible for a danger emanating from the very powers that they were resisting by sheltering Jews? It is not as if the parents had forced their children to fabricate bombs or to go out and kill Germans, in which case they would have made their children legitimate targets of war. The fact that the Germans were prepared to kill children for carrying on them other people's identity cards, or for simply being the children of rescuers of Jews, should be blamed on the Germans, not on the parents.

I believe this is the right argument here. It is not the parents' hiding of Jews that, by itself, may cause their children to be killed, but rather the Nazis' decision to kill all members of a family that is caught hiding Jews. Hence, between the parents' action to take in Jewish fugitives in their home, and the morally reprehensible outcome that their children are killed, there intervenes the action of the Nazis who deliberately carry out the killing of the children. And since this intervening action is the proximate sufficient cause of the children's death, it is the Nazis and the Nazis alone that should be held morally responsible. This is an application of *the principle of the intervening action*:

> According to this principle, when there is a causal connection between some person A's performing some action (or inaction) X [the parents' hiding Jews] and some other person C's incurring a certain harm Z [the children being killed], A's moral responsibility for Z is removed if, between X and Z, there intervenes some other action Y of some person B [the Nazis killing the children] who knows the relevant circumstances of his action and who intends to produce Z or who produces Z through recklessness. The reason for this removal is that B's intervening action Y is the more direct or proximate cause of Z and, unlike A's action (or inaction), Y is the sufficient condition of Z as it actually occurs. (Gewirth, 1982, p. 229; text in brackets added by the present author.)

When the parents decide to take the fugitives into their home, they are not doing anything morally wrong, but, on the contrary, they are doing something supererogatorily good. They are doing more than morality requires of them when they choose to protect the fugitives' right to life at the risk of having themselves and their children killed by the Germans. What they do is indeed "an act of grace" (Gewirth, 1978, p. 189). And the possibility that the aggressor may violate not only the fugitives' right to life, but also the parents' and their children's right to life, should not be allowed to shift the burden of moral blame and responsibility from the aggressor to the parents.

Hence, the heroism of responsibility manifested by the rescuers of Jews during World War II is morally justified in the sense that what they did are examples of supererogatory actions. That is, they went beyond the requirement of the *PGC* that we should act in accord with the generic rights of our recipients as well as of ourselves, by accepting a risk that they might be deprived of well-being in its most basic aspect, while trying to protect their recipients' right to that same most basic well-being. Hence, what they did cannot be required as a moral duty in the strict sense, but this should not detract from their actions the quality of being permeated by a morally justified heroism.

CHAPTER 9

Prudence and Courage

It is indeed a strange feeling to be soaring over the Arctic Ocean. The first one who has done it in a balloon. How soon will there be others to follow? Will they think of us as madmen, or will they follow our example? I cannot deny that the three of us are possessed by a proud feeling. We believe we may well accept death, having done what we have now done. Perhaps it is all a matter of an extremely strong sense of individuality which could not bear that we should live and die as rank and file men, forgotten by future generations. Is this vanity? [Det är ej så litet underligt att sväfva här öfver Polarhafvet. Den förste som i ballong sväfvat här. Huru snart skola vi väl få efterföljare? Skall man anse oss galna eller följa vårt exempel? Jag kan ej neka till att det är en stolt känsla som beherrskar oss alla tre. Vi mena att vi godt kunna taga döden sedan vi gjort det vi nu gjort. Månne ej det hela kommer sig af en ytterligt stark individualitetskänsla som ej kunnat fördraga att man skulle lefva och dö som en man i ledet, glömd af kommande slägten. Är detta äregirighet?] (Andrée, et al., pp. 393–394; my translation.)

These words were written by Salomon August Andrée on 12 July 1897, on the second day of the Swedish balloon expedition to the North Pole. The expedition included, in addition to Andrée himself, two other men, Knut Frænkel and Nils Strindberg. Theirs was the latest contribution to an ongoing competition between Scandinavian explorers to be the first to conquer the Arctic Pole. The Norwegian Fridtjof Nansen had recently returned after having failed to reach the Pole, and the Andrée expedition was, among other things, an expression of Swedish national pride and a willingness to distinguish oneself among the Nordic countries.

Nansen's plan had been to let his ship, the *Fram*, go as far north as possible on open waters, and then drift with the ice across the Arctic

Ocean. After having drifted like this for about a year and a half, Nansen together with a member of his crew left the ship and tried to reach the Pole by sledge. However, he was forced to give up and turn south, spending the winter on Franz Joseph Land. There he and his companion were picked up by a British ship, and they returned safely to Norway in August 1896, at just about the same time as *Fram* appeared with the rest of Nansen's crew. Although he had failed to reach the Pole, Nansen was widely acclaimed as a hero on his return.

Now, Andrée seems to have felt himself under some pressure to imitate and surpass the heroism of Nansen. But, being a modern-minded engineer, he also wanted to add something new to the field of Polar exploration, namely, the use of a hydrogen balloon as a means of transportation. The obvious difficulties involved in reaching the North Pole by water and ice, as witnessed by the Nansen expedition, made the idea of a balloon expedition all the more attractive. And as Andrée received financial support from celebrities such as Alfred Nobel (founder of the Nobel Prize) and King Oscar II, there seemed to be no obstacles to his plan. On the other hand, the fact that he got support from high places also made it increasingly difficult for Andrée to back down, should he, for one reason or another, come to doubt the success of the expedition.

Scheduled for the summer of 1896, the expedition was postponed for one year, due to unfavourable weather conditions. Then, in the autumn of 1896, came the decision of one of the participants, the meteorologist Nils Ekholm, to quit. Ekholm feared that the balloon cover was not sufficiently tight to hold its hydrogen for the time needed to take the expedition across the Arctic Ocean. He was replaced by Knut Frænkel.

As Andrée started his preparations the following spring, Fridtjof Nansen wrote to him, wishing him well on his journey, but also expressing his hope that

> you will, this time too, have the same courage and possess the same superiority to wait for the right moment and not go unless you find that it has come. I believe Macbeth's golden words could be written on your banner: "I dare do all that becomes a man, who dares do more is none." To draw this line is what real strength of

spirit is about. [De også denne gang har det samme mod og den samme overlegenhed til at afvente det gunstige öieblik og ikke gå uden De finder at dette er kommet, på Deres fane tror jeg Macbeths gyldne ord kunde stå: "I dare do all that becomes a man, who dares do more is none." Det er i at trække denne grendse den virkelige åndsstyrke viser sig.] (Andrée, et al., p. 68; my translation.)

But Andrée seems to have reached a point of no return. He thanked Nansen in a letter for his concern, adding that he was confident that Nansen would not blame him and his men "for what might happen", and that, although he once had shown himself capable of postponing his expedition, he now "very much desires to go" (Sundman, pp. 149–150). In an interview with a Norwegian newspaper, immediately before taking off from Svalbard, Andrée declared fatalistically that

> there is an old saying, that things never turn out as bad as you fear, and never as well as you hope. And I stick to that. I have no fear and no hope. [[E]t gammelt ord sier at det går aldri så dårligt som man frygter, og aldri så godt som man håper. Og til det holder jeg mig. Jeg eier ingen frygt og intet håp.] (Sundman, p. 179; my translation.)

When Andrée was speculating in his diary as to whether it was vanity that motivated him and his men, the balloon was in fact already down on the ice. Early on the second day (12 July 1897) of the expedition, it had drifted into a heavy mist which covered the balloon with a wet layer which, as it froze, pressed it down towards the ground. After a few hours of clear weather on 13 July, a fine rain started to fall, which soon consolidated in the shape of a new heavy layer of ice on the top of the balloon. On the morning of 14 July, Andrée and his men took down the balloon on the ice, as they feared that, in addition to the problem of keeping themselves in the air due to the layers of wet freezing on the top of the balloon, the winds might take them further out in the Arctic, but not across it. Andrée, Strindberg, and Frænkel now set out to cross the ice on foot, hauling sledges containing their instruments and supplies.

Their journey on the ice was to last for slightly more than three months, and ended in their death.

Their plan was to reach Franz Joseph Land, where Nansen had spent the winter of 1895–96. On the sledges, each of which carried a load of 160–200 kilograms, they had supplies for about six months, as well as a tent, a boat, and rifles and ammunition. The ice often proved a difficult road. Sometimes it would open in rifts and they were forced to make long detours, or to make dangerous crossings, ferrying their sledges on their boat across the rifts. Often the ice took the form not of a frozen plain, but of blocks and walls which proved very hard to pass. After only a few days' journey, Andrée and his men had to unload and abandon some of their supplies in order to facilitate the hauling of the sledges. They decided to try to supply themselves as they went along by hunting polar bears, seals, and various Arctic birds.

Soon they found out that the ice that they were travelling on did not drift south-east towards Franz Joseph Land, but rather in a south-west direction. They tried to compensate for this by going more to the east. They were slowed down, however, by the difficult terrain. It sometimes took them as much as ten hours to proceed two kilometres. Still, their spirits were rather high, and Andrée commented in his diary ironically on their unsuccessful attempts to keep themselves clean, and took pictures of their forks in order to document how they deteriorated as they were used on the meat of sinewy old polar bears. When one in the group asked if a certain rift could be passed easily, another retorted: "Yes, it can be easily done with difficulty" (Andrée, et al., p. 406).

However, in the face of the powerful ice-drift which, regardless of their efforts, took them farther away from their destination, Andrée decided to give up Franz Joseph Land and instead opt for Seven Islands, north of Svalbard. Here, as in the case of Franz Joseph Land, supplies were put in store for them beforehand, in the event that their balloon should have to go down.

As they continued to struggle against the ice-drift and the hardships of the terrain, signs of illness and fatigue began to appear in the group. On 28 August Andrée commented on the condition of Frænkel:

> F is weak again. Yesterday he was given a bit of opium for his diarrhea and this evening he was given a bit of morphine for his stomach-ache. Let us see if he will be a man again. [F är skral igen. Han fick igår en ruta opium mot diarrhén och har ikväll fått en ruta morfin mot magplågorna. Få se nu om han blir karl igen.] (Andrée, et al., p. 430; my translation.)

Just a few days later Andrée himself had to take both morphine and opium against similar symptoms. In addition to their intestinal problems, Frænkel's left foot was infected, and the other two men had to take turns in hauling his sledge, which, of course, slowed down the group. Once more they were overtaken by the ice-drift, and soon they had to give up reaching Seven Islands and Svalbard. Instead they were making plans for spending the winter on the ice. On 17 September Andrée laconically concluded in his diary: "Our position is not particularly good" ["Vår position är ej synnerligen god"] (Andrée, et al., p. 443). This seems to have been an understatement. After two months of difficult travelling on foot, they were not in the best possible condition to confront the Arctic winter. Choosing to camp on the ice also meant that they had to go with the ice-floes wherever they drifted.

However, in the spirit of their times, Andrée and his men did not let their present predicament get in the way of patriotic sentiment. On 18 September they celebrated the silver jubilee of King Oscar II, singing the national anthem under the union flag (Sweden and Norway were at the time united under the same monarch), toasting the king, and further solemnizing the occasion by sharing the fine port presented to them by the king before they left Sweden.

During the following days they built themselves an igloo on the ice. This was not to be their home for a long time, however, since the ice-floe rifted in the early hours of 2 October, threatening the igloo with immediate collapse and shattering their belongings as these now were spread on various parts of the original floe. Now they were forced to cross the ice-barriers surrounding the nearby White Island in order to get solid ground under their feet. Still, in the midst of their troubles, Andrée expressed his faith in his men in his diary:

Nobody had lost his courage. With fellows like these you should be able to manage under almost any circumstances. [Ingen hade förlorat modet. Med sådana kamrater bör man kunna reda sig under snart sagdt hvilka omständigheter som helst.] (Andrée, et al., p. 456; my translation.)

Likewise, Nils Strindberg's comment, "Exciting situation" ["Spännande situation"], does not express defeat or despair, but rather a readiness to take on whatever new challenges might come in his way.

Andrée and his men reached White Island on 5 October. From what remained of their diaries and notebooks when their final resting-place was discovered in 1930, we know that they had a hard time transporting their belongings from their first landing-place to the final camp-site higher up on the island. The last and barely legible entry in Andrée's diary mentions drift-wood (to be collected for a fire?) as well as a tent and a hut. Perhaps they were planning to build a hut or a new igloo, but this never took place. The last written message from the Andrée expedition is from Strindberg in his calendar, on 17 October. It just says "home, at 7.05 a.m." ["hem kl 7.5 f m"] (Andrée, et al., p. 464).

Nothing more was heard of Andrée and his men until the summer of 1930, when the Norwegian *Bratvaag* expedition went ashore on White Island and found the remains of the expedition. Andrée and Frænkel were found inside what once was the tent referred to in Andrée's last diary entry, made of varnished balloon silk. Strindberg was found in a crevice in the ground, about 30 metres from the tent. Obviously he had been the first to die, as he was the only one to be buried.

The exact cause of their death is hard to establish. At the time of their death they still possessed a fairly rich supply of meat, still to be found in 1930. They had rifles and ammunition and would hence have been able to hunt, should their supplies run out. Moreover, they did not lack either fuel or matches or wood to burn. Perhaps they simply froze to death, exhausted by hard labour and lack of rest.

Now, it would be hard to deny that Andrée and his men were courageous. They refused to give up even in the face of hard weather, difficult terrain, and the frustrating ice-drift which constantly deprived them of whatever progress they had hoped to make. Indeed, their struggle exemplifies an astonishingly powerful courage of creativity, as they refused for as long as they could to accept failed expectations as anything but challenges to renew their efforts. However, although we cannot question their courage, we may still question the *value* of their courage. Was the expedition really worth struggling and dying for? Would it not have been wiser for Andrée and his men to postpone their expedition once more, and so give themselves the opportunity to know more about what it would be like to fly a balloon over the Arctic?

Andrée, for instance, had claimed in 1895 that the meteorological conditions in the Arctic area were especially well suited for balloonists, since there would be very little precipitation, and that, due to the constant sunshine of the Arctic summer, whatever amount of snow might fall on the balloon would either melt away or be blown off by the wind (Andrée, 1895, pp. 67–68). However, instead of constant sunshine, Andrée and his men met with a constant fall of a fine rain which, in combination with a temperature close to freezing-point, came to cover the balloon with a coat of ice. It has been estimated (by K. A. B. Amundson and I. Malmer, in Andrée, et al., p. 134) that when the balloon was forced to the ground, the weight of its ice-coat must have been at least a ton.

Perhaps Andrée would not have found out the truth about the Arctic weather even if he had postponed his expedition a second time. After all, Nils Ekholm, the meteorologist who quit the expedition in 1896, did not object to Andrée's optimistic account of the effects of the sunny Arctic summer, and he was supposed to be an expert in this field. But Ekholm did quit the expedition, and his reason for doing so should have given Andrée cause for concern. Ekholm questioned Andrée's belief that the balloon would be sufficiently air-tight to take the expedition to the Pole and across the Arctic Ocean to populated areas in either North America or Northeast Asia. Andrée estimated that the balloon would be able to hold its hydrogen for at least 30 days, and that this would be more than enough for the expedition to be able to cross the Arctic Ocean. Ekholm, however, who carefully measured the daily loss of hydrogen as the balloon was anchored in a specially built house on Svalbard during the summer of 1896, found reason to doubt Andrée's optimism. And as Andrée did not seem to be interested in building a tighter balloon, Ekholm chose to quit.

As we know, the expedition failed not because of the balloon leaking hydrogen too fast, but because of the bad weather conditions of the Arctic. Still, Andrée's attitude to Ekholm's warnings seems to express a certain indifference as to whether his own estimates were accurate or not that is not consistent with responsible leadership. A more careful response would have been to reexamine not only the points brought to his attention by Ekholm regarding the tightness of the balloon, but also to subject his other assumptions to criticism, for instance, those regarding the Arctic weather. In his eagerness to try out his plan, Andrée seems not to have cared about critical objections. And this is what makes the whole project, including the courage manifested in it, liable to the *objection from prudence*: it does not take seriously the task of ascertaining that the persons involved are not subjected to any foreseeable and avoidable harm that is likely to diminish their capacity for future agency.

Now, this objection seems to be inconsistent with one of the central components of the courage of creativity, namely, the capacity for positive planning. The very essence of positive planning is that we should plan for success, not for failure, and that we should not be prevented from going ahead by the prospect of things going wrong. The objection from prudence, on the other hand, seems to insist that we should indeed make sure that nothing can go wrong, and that we should *not* proceed with our plans unless we can be assured that nothing bad will happen to us. The objection from prudence seems to blame Andrée for being a positive planner and, by implication, to question the rationality of the courage of creativity.

However, the tension between prudence and positive planning is, I believe, more apparent than real. It is a question of a difference in emphasis rather than of a logical contradiction. Positive planning is, as we should remind ourselves, indeed a form of *planning*, and as such it cannot do without the careful consideration of risks required by prudence. Positive planning should not be understood as a mindless optimism, dismissing all talk of risks regardless of the evidence at hand. Positive planning means that we should not give up our projects just because there is a possibility that they may fail. But this does not imply that we should *ignore* the possibility of failure. On the contrary, we should make our plans with a view to *neutralizing* that possibility, i.e., devise means to our end that eliminate or at least minimize the risk of failure. Hence, positive planning endorses a way of acting that is neither inhibited by the possibility of failure, nor negligent of that possibility.

Of course, if failure implies not only a temporary loss of resources that can be compensated for later, but the death or basic harm of the agent, it is all the more urgent that the agent's planning, as far as possible, takes care to minimize the possibility of failure. After all, the desired end is successful achievement, not suicide.

The courage of creativity, which is motivated by the agent's will to achieve, indeed presupposes prudential reasoning. In order to mobilize her determination to endure and overcome obstacles and so accomplish her projects, the agent must have a reasonable conception of the nature of these obstacles, as well as of what it takes to confront them. Hence, the courage of creativity can never condone a planning that substitutes optimism for thoroughness. Positive planning indeed involves an agency-related optimism – this is the meaning of *positive* planning – but it is also about *planning*, that is, a careful consideration of what means are necessary and efficient to the achievement of the desired end. We should plan for successful achievement, not for failure and disaster, but all the same we are supposed to *plan*.

Was Andrée lacking in prudence in the sense relevant to the discussion of the courage of creativity? And if so, does this mean that he did not possess that form of courage after all?

Now, we should guard ourselves against the fallacy of inferring from the fact that Andrée's expedition ended in tragedy, that he must have been imprudent in his planning. Failure does not by itself imply a lack of prudence. A project may fail due to events that could not have been predicted by any reasonably prudent planner, such as accidents, or the evil projects of other people of which the agent may know nothing. (As I write these lines, the world is still shaken by the terrorist attack on the World Trade Center in New York. Certainly, none of those innocent airline passengers who were killed as the terrorists steered the two planes into the WTC towers, thereby killing thousands of other innocent people in the building and on the ground, could be blamed for imprudent planning although their choice of means of transportation ended in their death. They had no reason whatsoever to include the possibility of a terrorist attack in their travel planning.)

On the other hand, the success of a particular project is not necessarily an indication of prudent planning. Even imprudent planners may succeed, due to sheer luck, or to the unexpected intervention and assistance of other people, or to an unpredicted change in external conditions. (If the Arctic weather conditions had been better and Andrée had been able to return to civilization, would we still have been discussing his expedition as a possible example of imprudent planning?)

In a speech delivered to the Royal Swedish Academy of Science as well as to the Swedish Society for Anthropology and Geography in February 1895, Andrée himself discusses the possible impact of the Arctic summer weather on a balloon expedition. He notes the objection that "a voyage like this one could be completely destroyed by a single snowfall, burdening the balloon with, e.g., 30 kilogrammes of snow per square metre" ["en sådan resa som denna skulle kunna alldeles omintetgöras genom ett enda snöfall, som belastade ballongen med t. ex. 30 kilogram snö pr kvadratmeter"] (Andrée, 1895, p. 67). While admitting that such a snowfall would indeed be disastrous, should it occur, Andrée quickly goes on to assure his audience that "this will not happen, since not even the *sum total* of the precipitation during June, July, and August amounts to 30 kilogrammes per square metre, and the precipitation during that month – July – in which the voyage should be made, does not amount to more than 6.8 kilogrammes per square metre" ["att detta icke kommer att inträffa, ty icke ens *summan* af nederbörden under juni, juli och augusti uppgår till 30 kilogram pr kvadratmeter, och nederbörden för den månad – juli – , då resan bör göras, uppgår ej till mer än 6,8 kilogram pr kvadratmeter"] (Andrée, 1895, p. 68).

Andrée adds that "the snow or ice that possibly may be gathered on the balloon is subjected to an evaporation which in these parts and at this time of the year will remove 2 or 3 times as much moisture as is contained in the precipitation" ["den snö eller is, som möjligen samlas på ballongen, är utsatt för afdunstning, som i dessa trakter och vid denna årstid aflägsnar 2 à 3 gånger så mycken fuktighet, som nederbörden utgör"] (ibid.).

The figures referred to by Andrée regarding estimated evaporation emanated from the observations made by Swedish and American expeditions to the Arctic area in 1882–83. However, from these observations it would be possible to derive less auspicious conclusions for a prospective balloon expedition than Andrée did. In fact, the meteorologist Nils Ekholm provides in a speech given to the Swedish Society for Anthropology and Geography at the same time (and while he still intended to participate in Andrée's expedition) pieces of information that should have caused some concern. While agreeing with Andrée's view of summer evaporation in the Arctic, Ekholm notes the effects of this evaporation on the weather conditions: "Mist is frequent at the fringes of the polar basin, wherever the melting polar ice meets warm water" ["Dimma är vanlig vid polarbäckenets kanter, öfverallt där den smältande polarisen möter varmt vatten"] (Ekholm, p. 213).

Moreover, Ekholm refers to certain observations, not mentioned by Andrée, made by the previous expeditions, regarding the incidence of clouds in the Arctic region: "The amount of clouds seems to be greater than in our parts during summer" ["Molnmängden synes vara större än i våra trakter under sommaren"]. Ekholm, however, tries to present this fact in as bright colours as possible, noting that "[e]ven during such an unfavourable month as July 1882 at Fort Conger, still 15 per cent of the sky was cloudless" ["Äfven under en så ogynnsam månad som juli 1882 vid Fort Conger voro dock 15 % af himmelen molnfria"] (p. 213).

Given these reports of mist and clouds, Andrée should have had reason to be somewhat less confident about "the permanent sunlight" in the Arctic. In his 1895 speech Andrée referred to

> those great advantages which emanate from the fact that, during the entire time of the voyage, the sun is above the horizon. Thereby darkness is prevented from depriving the aviators of knowledge of the features of the surrounding landscape.... The permanent sunlight also benefits the aviators by keeping the temperature of the balloon and

the air exceptionally stable, so that there will be little variability in the carrying capacity of the balloon. [[D]e stora fördelar, som härflyta däraf, att solen hela restiden befinner sig öfver horisonten. Därigenom förhindras, att mörker undanrycker luftseglarne kännedomen om beskaffenheten af det omgifvande landskapet.... Det ständiga solskenet gör luftseglarne nytta också därigenom att det håller ballong- och lufttemperaturen synnerligen jämn, så att ballongens bärkraft blir föga variabel.] (Andrée, 1895, pp. 66–67; my translation.)

Perhaps Andrée expected conditions to be better closer to the Pole than at the fringes of the polar region where the previous expeditions had collected their data. But in order for him to get to the Pole, he would still have to fly through mist and clouds. And it should have occurred to him that although evaporation, under favourable circumstances, perhaps could remove twice as much moisture as was contained in the precipitation, things might be different should there be no sunshine.

By choosing to interpret the observations made by the earlier expeditions in a way that would support the idea of a balloon expedition to the North Pole, and ignoring equally reasonable interpretations that would imply a less encouraging view of such a venture, Andrée (but also Ekholm) in fact violates the requirement of prudence. That is, Andrée does not take seriously the task of ascertaining that he and the other members of his expedition are not subjected to any foreseeable and avoidable harm that is likely to diminish their capacity for future agency. Andrée was aware of the objection that precipitation may force the balloon down on the ground, but he chose to disregard it on account of the "permanent sunlight" in the Arctic region and the expected effects of evaporation. In so doing he ignored the observed fact that mist and clouds were frequent features of the Arctic summer, which, in combination with a temperature near freezing-point, should point to an obvious risk that there would be a layer of ice covering the balloon.

Now, this does not entail that Andrée and his men were not courageous. On the contrary, the persistence and endurance manifested in their efforts to survive during the months following their landing on the ice, clearly indicate that they were not inclined to give up easily. Even in the face of the insurmountable powers of the ice-drift and the merciless lot of being left to themselves in the inhospitable Arctic climate, they did not sulk or complain, nor did they give themselves over to anger or despair. Instead they acted constructively, doing their best to overcome the obstacles at hand, determined to struggle on. They did not succeed, but it would constitute a grave injustice to their memory to deny that they possessed the courage of creativity.

However, it is one thing to be courageous, and another to be *justified* in one's courage. As we have already noted, villains may possess the courage of conviction, but the fact that we call them villains implies that we do not believe their courageous behaviour to be morally justified. Now, while the courage of conviction is related to the agent's sense of moral responsibility and to purposes that can be evaluated from a *moral* point of view, the courage of creativity, being related to the agent's will to achieve and to the furtherance of her personal purposes, can be assessed from a *prudential* point of view. Hence, just as we may distinguish between the claim that an agent possesses the courage of conviction and the claim that her courage is morally justified, so we may distinguish between the claim that an agent possesses the courage of creativity and the claim that her courage is prudentially justified.

Since the value of the courage of creativity is related to the prudential purpose of promoting the agent's personal good, a prudentially justified application of this form of courage should not lead to the agent's suffering a harm that decreases her ability to pursue her personal good in the future. From the point of view of the agent's personal good, it is essential that she maintains and even increases her capacity for agency, and so enables herself to transform her will to achieve into long-term successful action. Regardless of the various conceptions of their personal good that different agents may entertain, they will all need to be able to maintain as well as to increase their capacity for agency, since it is by their *actions* that they will try to realize their various projects. Hence, knowingly risking to diminish one's capacity for future agency (not to speak of knowingly risking to completely remove that capacity), just for the sake of realizing a particular goal, cannot be prudentially justified.

In order for her to further her personal good, the agent should take a long-term view of her agency, trying steadily to improve her capacity for purpose-fulfilment and so enable herself to satisfy her will to achieve over a complete lifetime. Here Aristotle's dictum applies, that "[o]ne swallow does not make a summer; neither does one day. Similarly neither can one day, or a brief space of time, make a man blessed and happy" (Aristotle, 1098a8–27, p. 76). It is this long-term perspective that is upheld by the requirement of prudence, when it prescribes that we should take seriously the task of ascertaining that, as we try to achieve a particular purpose of ours, we are not subjected to any foreseeable and avoidable harm that will diminish our capacity for future actions. And it is because of his neglect of this requirement that Andrée's courage of creativity cannot be prudentially justified.

For an illustration of a prudentially justified instance of the courage of creativity, we might consider Roald Amundsen's 1911–12 Antarctic expedition, the successful outcome of which was that Amundsen became the first man to conquer the South Pole. Unlike his rival in the race for the South Pole, Sir Robert Scott, the Norwegian Amundsen was eager to adapt to environmental conditions and to benefit from the experiences of previous polar explorers and from the ways of life of the arctic Eskimos. On 20 October 1911 Amundsen and four of his men set out on skis, leaving the coast base camp Framheim, with fifty-two Greenland dogs to pull four sledges with provisions. About one month later they began the difficult transition to the polar plateau, crossing the Transantarctic Mountains. Having successfully ascended to the plateau, twenty-four of the dogs were slaughtered to feed the men and the remaining dogs. Some of the meat was stored in a depot to be consumed by the expedition on the way back. On 14 December 1911 they arrived at the South Pole, and four days later they started their journey back to Framheim where they arrived on 26 January 1912, now with only eleven dogs still alive. They had spent ninety-nine days travelling a total distance of about 3,000 kilometres. (For a recent account of Amundsen's expedition, see Bomann-Larsen, pp. 165–169.)

Amundsen's capacity for prudent planning can be clearly seen when his methods are contrasted with those of his rival, Sir Robert

Scott. For one thing, Amundsen took care not to exhaust his men and the dogs. Scott, who relied on ponies, was not as wise:

> Scott's men and ponies trudged eight hours and more to cover ten to thirteen miles a day; Amundsen's daily stage of fifteen to twenty miles was done in five or six hours with plenty in reserve, and nothing to do but eat and sleep – especially sleep – for the rest of the day.... Like a long distance runner, Amundsen started slowly and evenly to nurse his strength for the last lap. His men and dogs knew that they would do a certain regular amount of work each day, to set off fresh on the morrow. Scott was not quite so self-controlled. He had a Dionysian urge to show off his undoubted physical strength and drive his companions to exhaustion. He did not believe that a day's work had been done unless there was visible distress. (Huntford, p. 430.)

Amundsen's ambition to win the race for the South Pole never interfered with his sense of responsibility and prudence. He consistently planned and acted to have a reassuring margin of safety. In this too, he was unlike Scott:

> On his departure from 82° S., Amundsen carried supplies for a hundred days, taking him to February 6th, 1912. According to his timetable, *and on his performance so far*, he would return to Framheim by January 31st. This meant that even in the unlikely event of missing all depots laid so far, he could still reach the Pole, return to Framheim, turn around, and do another hundred miles to the south before his food gave out. He had three or four times as much paraffin as he needed. He allowed one day in four for rest and bad weather.... Scott, by comparison, had allowed no margin of safety in food, fuel or weather. Simple figures make the point. When Amundsen started, he had three tons of supplies in his depots; Scott had one ton. There were five in Amundsen's party, making 1,300 pounds per man; Scott started with seventeen men which meant 124 pounds per head. Amundsen had ten times more food and fuel per man than Scott. For Scott to miss a single depot would be fatal. (Huntford, p. 434.)

Amundsen's use of dogs that both could pull the sledges and serve as food, reveals his ability to adapt to the conditions at hand, as does his selection of Eskimo reindeer fur clothing (Huntford, p. 348) to protect himself and his men from the cold. His foresight contrasted with the rather arrogant form of ignorance exemplified by Scott. He too had brought dogs with him, but he did not assign to them the same major role that Amundsen did. Instead he relied on ponies and motor sledges. The motor sledges, however, broke down and could not be repaired, since neither tools nor sufficient spares had been brought along. And then there were the ponies:

> The ponies alone, totally unsuited to the conditions, fighting their way into the drift, their nearest food growing 2,000 miles away, bear witness to Scott's inability to grasp the implications of the cold, storms and unpredictable surfaces of the Antarctic world.... For at least four years he had known he would return to the Antarctic. He could have visited Norway or the Alps; learnt to ski and drive dogs himself; acquired a grounding in the internal combustion engine, (he was, after all, a torpedo expert) or even tried some mountaineering. He had done none of these things. Incompetent design penetrated into most details of equipment. Scott had learned nothing and forgotten nothing. He still used neither furs nor anoraks, but wore the same inefficient garments with separate hoods that had disfigured the *Discovery* expedition [to the Antarctic in 1901–02]. His tents, without sewn-in groundsheets, slipped over a cumbrous framework of poles, like a tepee, were difficult to erect in a gale. And where transport was concerned, Scott trusted neither ponies, nor skis, dogs or sledge; in truth all he really believed in was human effort. (Huntford, p. 423.)

Scott seems to have despised the idea of depending on dogs. In fact, he had made it clear that

> no journey ever made with dogs can approach the height of the fine conception which is realised when a party of men go forth to face hardships, dangers and difficulties with their own unaided efforts. (Quoted in Huntford, p. 465.)

Accordingly, as Scott and his men began their ascent to the polar plateau, the worn-out ponies were shot while the dog team were sent back to the British base camp. Scott seemed to have enjoyed the prospect of man-hauling all his loads up to the heights, believing in "a code of behaviour in which doing things the hard way was virtue in itself" (Huntford, p. 465). However, his way of leading the British expedition brought a terrible pressure on his men:

> Scott possessed great physical courage and phenomenal stamina. One of his weaknesses as a leader was to expect the same powers in everyone and ignore the differences in men. Beyond this, he was a man who always raced; against a rival, a friend, and, in the last resort against himself.... On the march, Scott had an irrational, almost sadistic love of driving his companions to exhaustion. On the borders of survival, such men are dangerous. Amundsen's companions knew that when they had done their fifteen or twenty miles, they stopped, outspanned and camped. There was rhythm, regularity, discipline, certainty, finite compass to their days. Whatever his *angst* over being forestalled, Amundsen had the intelligence and self-control to filter his emotions and avoid driving his men to the limit. Scott, with manic urge, drove his followers on, whatever the consequences. (Huntford, pp. 468–469.)

According to Huntford, "Scott wanted to be a hero; Amundsen merely wanted to get to the Pole" (p. 496). It is perhaps in this difference of motivation that we should look for a distinction between those traits of character that are favourable to prudent planning, and those that are not. The very ambition to be a hero may easily give support to a certain recklessness when it comes to taking care of foreseeable risks. The heroism exemplified by Scott (and possibly also by Andrée) is the heroism of honour. The hero of honour, as depicted in chapter 8, desires social recognition for his ability to confront great dangers, emphasizing his willingness to die, rather than the importance of the end for which he is risking his life. In the end, this may well carry the implication that the hero of honour cares more about dying an "honourable" death, than about being successful in his enterprise. Scott seems to answer to that description, while Amundsen subordinates whatever desire for social recognition he might have had to the successful realization of his expedition. Andrée, on the other hand, seems to be more like Scott, when he claimed, speaking not only for himself, but also for his men (whom he did not ask for their opinion in the matter), that "we may well accept death, having done what we have now done".

And, like Andrée and his men, Scott and all those who had followed him had to pay with their lives for ignoring the requirement of prudence. Returning from the South Pole, having arrived there more than a month later than Amundsen, Scott and his men had to man-haul their remaining sledge, exhausted, and lacking sufficient provisions:

> They had to drive themselves so many miles a day to reach the next depot before supplies gave out. Their already minimal rations were reduced to spin them out, and by now they were probably down to little more than half the food they needed. To do their distances they had to drag their sledge for anything up to twelve hours out of the twenty-four at an altitude of 10,000 feet; a strain on healthy men. One can safely do without either food or rest in emergencies, but to deprive oneself of both is to ask too much of Nature. (Huntford, pp. 518–519.)

Starving and ill-clothed, short on fuel, and possibly afflicted by scurvy, due to vitamin C deficiency, Scott and his companions were soon to meet their end. At some time late in March 1912, they were all dead, Scott leaving several farewell letters on his body, in which he repeatedly comes back to the theme of heroic death. In one of them he notes that "[w]e are showing that Englishmen can still die with a bold spirit, fighting it out to the end", and in another that "we shall die like gentlemen" (quoted in Huntford, p. 543).

In his biography of Amundsen and Scott, Roland Huntford concludes that Scott was entirely responsible for the disaster of his expedition:

> Scott had worn his men out on the climb, without thinking of the return. In any case, by his basic decision to man-haul, he had

graphically proved Nansen's point that "taking dogs is cruel, but it is also cruel to overburden human beings with work". That Scott faced temperatures between five and ten degrees lower than Amundsen was his own fault. By taking ponies and consequently delaying his start, he had made certain of being on the Plateau three weeks after the summer solstice and the turn of the season. Low temperature was a strain he could ill afford. Excepting mittens and boots, Scott had no furs, the absence of which around the face was enough to explain some of the party's persistent frostbite. Poor skiing technique, unintelligent navigation, a badly-loaded, ill-maintained and ill-running sledge, inefficient camping routine, the disruptions caused by the last-minute addition of a fifth man; the list of defects was comprehensive. Scott had been so consistently inept as to almost suggest the workings of a death wish. (Huntford, p. 509.)

Not only was Scott a less prudent and efficient leader of an expedition than Amundsen, but he also lacked Amundsen's flexible and adaptive approach to the polar environment:

Amundsen knew that it was stupid to kick against the pricks. He had a proper humility before Nature, accepting a rough justice in her dictates. He knew that if it snows today it will be hard crust tomorrow; that after the storm skiing is good; that a blizzard is a time to rest. Scott, by contrast, expected the elements to be ordered for his benefit, and was resentful each time he found that they were not. This was a manifestation of the spiritual pride that was Scott's fatal flaw. (Huntford, p. 429.)

The lesson brought home by the cases of Amundsen and Scott is that an agent's confidence in her powers of agency should always be backed up by an actual *competence* on her part regarding the task at hand. And it is this competence that the requirement of prudence is meant to secure. In the words of Amélie Oksenberg Rorty:

The best preparation for courageous action is the preparation for action: competence and confidence in competence. Dangerous and

> fearful actions form a heterogeneous class, with distinctive problems of attention and competence. But competence is always specific and confidence without competence is folly. Often the skills of the courageous are those of proper focusing, cognitive habits specific to the actions they must perform. (Rorty, p. 161.)

Hence, the courage of creativity should never be divorced from its prudential justification, just as the courage of conviction should never be divorced from its moral justification. While it is *morally* important that the beliefs for which one is prepared to kill and be killed indeed are justified in accordance with universally valid and rational principles, it is *prudentially* important that the agent's desire for successful purpose-fulfilment does not involve her in projects which actually will entail a diminished capacity for purpose-fulfilment on her part. The value of the courage of creativity is basically prudential, consisting in its enhancement of the agent's personal good by means of sustaining and increasing her capacity for successful agency. It is to make sure that the courage of creativity really will have this prudentially valuable outcome that we need the constraints of the requirement of prudence.

CHAPTER 10

Some Concluding Reflections on Courage

In this concluding chapter, we will further clarify our analysis of the meaning and importance of courage. We will proceed by taking care of certain residual questions, relating to our discussion so far. These questions focus on certain allegedly problematic aspects of courage which may seem to invalidate the conclusion that it is indeed a desirable virtue. We will examine these questions in the form of three objections to the idea that courage is valuable.

The Objection Regarding Courage as a Form of Sexism

This is the objection that courage is an expression of male self-idolatry, according to which men should be not only fearless, but dominant. Courage, the objection continues, is closely related to ideas of virility and potency. Hence, to cultivate courage is, at least implicitly, to affirm a sexist view of the world, in which men are praised for just "being men" and for their capacity for domination. In the words of N. J. H. Dent:

> [The courageous man] dominates his situation and unflinchingly drives through to his objectives; he makes things go the way *he* wants. Thus we see that courage is an exhibition of power, strength and force of will and character; cowardice of impotence, weakness and feebleness of will and character. And it is to it as this mark of manly strength, this potent domination and command of circumstances, of people and events, that we should look to find a source for the idea that courage is as such an excellence in a man.... We must not forget that we have the word 'virtue' from the Latin *vir*,

> which forms the root also of 'virility'. Virility (which, of course, covers more than sexual potency) is the mark of manly excellence; and this the man of courage above all possesses. (Dent, p. 575.)

Dent argues that this conception of courage is "sexist" and substantiates her claim by noting that cowardice is associated with "effeminacy" (p. 576). However, while this represents *one* possible understanding of courage, we should be careful not to conclude that it is the only one, nor that it is the most reasonable one. For one thing, we should note that Dent slides between a neutral and an aggressive interpretation of the concept of courage. On the one hand, she depicts courage as a "strength and force of will and character", and this it certainly is. But by accepting this description we have not committed ourselves to any particular position regarding to what use the courageous agent must put her strength and force of will and character. The courageous agent indeed possesses a power of agency which the coward does not, as she is able to confront her fears of failure and personal transience and carry on with her plans and projects. But this power, taken by itself, is neutral. It could be used for good as well as for bad purposes, to realize a difficult but peaceful project as well as to participate in a war of aggression.

However, Dent goes on to suggest an aggressive interpretation of the courageous agent's power of agency, by describing it as "potent domination" and "command of circumstances, of people and events". The courageous agent is depicted as not merely possessing a greater capacity for agency than the non-courageous agent, but as a Nietzschean overman with dictatorial inclinations. And, clearly, this aggressive interpretation should not be elevated into *the* interpretation of courage. Compare, for instance, those heroes of responsibility who rescued Jews during World War II, many of whom were women, with a dictator like Benito Mussolini, who indeed cultivated an image of himself as both potent (in all senses of that term) and dominant. The power of agency of the rescuers is manifested in a certain self-control, necessary to the carrying out of a difficult and dangerous undertaking, rather than in an urge to dominate others. As Eva Fogelman notes:

> A core confidence, a strong sense of self, and a supportive situation had allowed bystanders to undertake the rescue. But once the decision to help had been reached and the rescue had begun, a different self – a *rescuer self* – emerged, to do what had to be done and to keep rescuers from becoming overwhelmed by new responsibilities and pressures. (Fogelman, p. 68.)

From her interviews with surviving rescuers, Fogelman concluded that, contrary to her own anticipations, women were as much involved in dangerous activities as men:

> Running through all these various inquiries [of previous researchers] was the assumption, sometimes implicit, sometimes overt, that in dangerous situations men would be more likely to help. I too assumed that women would undertake less physically taxing or hazardous tasks and leave the heroics to men. Time and again I was proven wrong. Women told of how they had acted as decoys, couriers, double agents, and border runners. Women such as Czechoslovakian historian Vera Laska were an integral part of both resistance and rescue work. Laska was a Czech resistance fighter who also led Jews and other fugitives to safety in Yugoslavia. German patrols made these border crossings extremely dangerous. (Fogelman, pp. 242–243.)

In fact, judging from Fogelman's account, the real sexist prejudice is not so much holding that courage is an "excellence in a man", as denying that this excellence is shared also by women.

> Given the opportunity, women proved to be good spies, smugglers, and saboteurs. Yet their deeds were largely overlooked. In the postwar celebration of men's daring deeds, the quiet bravery of women was ignored. The traditional hero was a swashbuckling male, and heroes who did not fit that model were ignored. (Fogelman, p. 244.)

Very different from the self-controlling courage of the rescuers is the exhibitionist courage of Benito Mussolini, who, as a soldier in

World War I, refused chloroform when undergoing a painful operation to remove shell splinters lodged in his body. As Mussolini's biographer Jasper Ridley observes, the reason for his rejection of an anaesthetic was probably that "he wished to demonstrate his heroism to himself and to those who watched him" (Ridley, p. 79). Moreover, as dictator of Italy Mussolini seemed to have taken a certain pleasure in exercising a virile domination of the kind that Dent wants to identify courage with:

> Like Napoleon, his only sensual pleasure was sex. He had always had love affairs, perhaps because they satisfied his lust for power. He believed that the masses, like women, admired masterful men. Mussolini enjoyed seducing and mastering women, but he enjoyed even more seducing and mastering the masses. (Ridley, p. 170.)

Now, while Mussolini's demonstration of bravado and potency may well fit Dent's classification of courage as dominating manliness, it is just as clear that the courage of the rescuers was of a different kind. Moreover, there are women who manifest the courage Dent associates with men, assuming "command of circumstances, of people and events". Think of, for instance, Joan of Arc, who, at the age of seventeen, in obedience to what she experienced as the voices of saints and angels, raised the English siege of Orléans, and enabled the disinherited Charles VII of France to be crowned in Reims in 1429. Sustained by her religious conviction, Joan manifested the courage of a soldier and fought for what she perceived to be a just cause. (For the significance of Joan's involvement in French politics, see Wood, 1988.)

Likewise, throughout history we find women who, disguised as men, join armies as soldiers and freely subject themselves to the hardships of military life and war. Ulrika Eleonora Stålhammar, a Swedish woman, left her home in 1713, at the age of twenty-four, dressed herself as a man and adopted the name of Wilhelm Edstedt. After having spent a couple of years working as a servant, she joined the army in 1715 and remained in military service until 1726, meanwhile marrying another woman. The whole affair was disclosed as she decided to reconnect with her family. Reappearing as a woman, Stålhammar had to explain her long absence, and in a letter to the legal authorities she asked for their forgiveness. From the legal point of view, the most damaging aspect of her behaviour was that she had married another woman, thereby having deceived and mocked the church. However, as it was testified that Stålhammar's married life had been "godfearing, virtuous, and loving", the court adopted a lenient approach, and she got away with a month in prison. At least two other cases of Swedish women impersonating male soldiers are known from the same period. (See Österberg, pp. 267–283.)

Similarly, James McPherson refers in passing to "the several hundred women who managed to enlist as soldiers in the [American] Civil War" (p. 65). It is at least probable that these women must have possessed some of that capacity for commanding circumstances and events that Dent tends to identify with a male conception of courage.

Moreover, to the extent that men and women come to share similar conditions in times of war, it seems as if their reactions and attitudes also tend to be similar. The British feminist Vera Brittain, who served as a nurse during World War I, recalled that she and her colleagues, after having assisted in surgical operations, "were able to drink tea and eat cake in the theatre … in that foetid stench, … the saturated dressings and yet more gruesome human remnants heaped on the floor" (quoted in Kent, p. 62).

Rather than having male bravery opposed to female softness, the experience of war seems to unite men and women at the front in a shared sense of vulnerability, and in an effort to cope with extreme circumstances which they can never wholly control:

> Women at the front or in positions that approximated those of the frontsoldiers shared with the men experiences denied to those at home. Rather than construe men in fantastic terms, derived from a different construction of war given in patriotic journalism, government propaganda, and sanitized letters home, feminists at the front had an understanding of men's experiences and of men that was far more in keeping with those of the men themselves.… Their familiarity with what men suffered led them to think of the

> male of the species not as some barbaric, destructive creature who could not control his most violent instincts, but as a hurt, pathetic, vulnerable, patient, childlike victim of circumstances far beyond his control. The sexual imagery utilized to depict or represent the war, consequently, involved a much greater sense of partnership, of participation on equal terms, of fellowship with men, than did that of the home front. (Kent, p. 72.)

Now, we should not deny that there is indeed a male *cult* of courage in the sense indicated by Dent. The injunction "Be a man!" expresses a male self-image that connotes manhood with courage, stamina, and mental as well as physical strength. However, the fact that men may have endeavoured to *cultivate* and *exhibit* courage does not imply that courage by definition is a male attribute. Moreover, courage as it is analysed in this study, is not conceived of as an exclusively martial virtue. On the contrary, the courage of creativity, as we have described it above, denotes an agency-related optimism that has nothing to do with a capacity for "potent domination", but rather with the persistent struggle to make the most of the situation at hand, given the agent's purposes and abilities. And the courage of conviction, in the form that is defended in the present work, expresses the agent's sense of moral responsibility, motivating her to confront her fear of personal transience, not for the sake of "dominating" others, but for the sake of assisting persons in desperate need and to help them free themselves from the domination of their oppressors. And, as the case of the rescuers of Jews indicates, women as well as men may prove themselves courageous as they provide such help and assistance. Hence, the objection regarding sexism fails to apply to courage as described and defended in the present study.

The Objection Regarding Courage as a Cultivation of Insensitivity

> The magnetizing cognitive dispositions of courage seem typically to exclude, or at any rate to diminish the force of other categorial dispositions. The courageous are normally not magnetized to aesthetic

delight in the ludicrous, to wonder, or emphatic identification. The confidence that is part of courage tends to dampen imaginative foresight directed to avoiding oppositional confrontation. Perceiving actions as victories or defeats, seeing compromise as a partial loss, the courageous do not usually promote, and often resist, cooperative, compromising attitudes…. Though it may take courage to question one's ends, the courageous normally accept the goods they serve without question. (Rorty, pp. 154–155.)

Rorty's criticism seems to be inspired by an assumption that courage is primarily a martial virtue, preparing and enabling the agent to fight by reducing the options at hand (and thereby removing the restraints on action that hesitation may bring) to the apocalyptic alternatives of either total victory or total defeat. However, the view of courage elaborated in this study does not endorse any such reductionism. On the contrary, the courage of creativity enjoins the agent to adopt a constructive attitude to the situation at hand, making the most of the opportunities that it contains, rather than obsessively clinging to a predetermined course of action with no regard for possible alternatives. Likewise, the courage of conviction, which is motivated by the agent's sense of moral responsibility, should not be understood as an exercise in uncompromising and uncritical obedience to a sacred cause. Of course, as the example of Maximilien Robespierre suggests, *some* courageous people do have this uncompromising disposition. But there is no necessary connection between the courage of conviction and the kind of fanaticism depicted by Rorty. In this context, it is important that we remind ourselves of the distinction between the kind of courage of conviction that is morally justified, and the kind that is not.

A morally justified courage of conviction should be consistent with the reasoning of the objective agent-self, from whose point of view a person will identify herself as just one agent among others, sharing with all other agents certain rights and duties regarding the generic goods of agency. Hence, an agent exercising a morally justified courage cannot adopt the uncompromising stance criticized by Rorty. On the contrary, the rights of other agents will always set limits to what she is entitled to do in the pursuit of her personal ends as well as ends relating to the common good. Hence, an agent has no right to deliberately sacrifice the lives of innocent persons, not even for the sake of maintaining the institutions of a morally justified civic community (although she may have to accept that innocent persons will be killed as an unintended effect of a necessary and morally justified act of war or resistance). And even soldiers in the midst of a war may recognize the limits set to their actions by the rights of other persons, as World War I soldier Frank Richards testifies:

> When bombing dug-outs or cellars, it was always wise to throw the bombs into them first and have a look around them after. But we had to be very careful in this village as there were civilians in some of the cellars. We shouted down to them to make sure. Another man and I shouted down one cellar twice and receiving no reply were just about to pull the pins out of our bombs when we heard a woman's voice and a young lady came up the cellar steps … She and the members of her family … had not left [the cellar] for some days. They guessed an attack was being made and when we first shouted down had been too frightened to answer. If the young lady had not cried out when she did, we would have innocently murdered them all. (Quoted in Walzer, p. 152.)

As Michael Walzer notes, commenting on this case, the good soldier should not only adhere to the negative principle of not intentionally killing or harming non-combatants, but also, as Frank Richards did, adhere to the positive principle of actively trying to minimize non-combatant casualties (Walzer, pp. 155–156.) Hence, far from being deprived of "imaginative foresight", soldiers, possessing a morally justified courage of conviction, will expose themselves to an additional danger for the sake of not bringing death and destruction on the innocent. As Frank Richards observed, if he was to act only with his personal safety in mind, he should have thrown his bomb into the cellar without calling first. After all, if there had been German soldiers down there, they could have stormed out and killed Richards where he stood, bomb in hand, waiting for a reply. A just war, however, requires of its soldiers discrimination as well as courage, and there is no need to assume that the one by necessity should exclude the other.

Far from being inconsistent with psychological dispositions such as empathy and sensibility, the morally justified courage of conviction rests on a sense of moral responsibility, presupposing that the agent is capable of identifying with the important interests and agency-related right-claims of other people. The morally just courageous person is not monomanically attached to the idea of victory, regardless of the costs. On the contrary, her sense of moral responsibility will make her reject certain possible easy victories, because of their negative impact on the basic rights of other agents.

The Objection Regarding Courage as Incapable of Dealing with Tragedy

According to this objection, the theory of courage developed in this study cannot help a person to confront tragedy, since tragedy cannot be opposed either by our will to achieve or by our sense of moral responsibility. Here the terms "tragedy" and "tragic events" denote the occurrence of disasters and deprivations that appear to be causally as well as morally undeserved, in the sense that they cannot be seen as either an expected causal effect of a person's actions or omissions, or as a retribution for past wrongdoing. We may not be surprised to hear that a person who habitually races with other car-drivers on the highway is suddenly killed in a car accident, or that a murderer has been killed by the son of one of his victims. We may regret these events, but we can perceive a certain causal and moral logic in them. Racing with other car-drivers as well as killing other people clearly increase the risk that the agent of these activities will meet with a violent death, in an accident or as the victim of an act of revenge. But there are disasters and deprivations that cannot be accounted for as causally or morally deserved in this sense. Their existence is familiar to us, since

> we know that life is not fair, that misfortunes befall the innocent and the virtuous, that children are killed in natural disasters, that people die "before their time" and sometimes on the very brink of

an elusive success, that villains often flourish and sometimes get away with murder. (Solomon, p. 118.)

Think of, for instance, people who have been born blind, or who, in spite of their having taken care not to indulge in harmful practices, such as smoking, die of cancer or from a stroke while still fairly young. Or think of people who, in spite of their being nice and friendly, yet cannot find the love that they desperately seek, and have to live and die alone. These are instances of tragedy, and it indeed seems as if neither the will to achieve, nor a sense of moral responsibility could help a person to confront such tragedies, or even the fear of being a victim of them.

To mobilize the will to achieve is not very helpful, since it is not a question of successful *achievement* whether we should avoid getting cancer or whether we should experience love. Of course, we may increase the ratio of vegetables in our food, intending to promote our health, and we may take dancing lessons to improve our chances of finding romance. But while we may achieve a healthy *diet* and succeed in becoming a good *dancer*, we cannot tell whether we have thereby also achieved lasting good *health* or whether we will actually be *loved*. It is not like studying for an exam, or learning a new language, where we can have a fairly definite idea of what it will take to be successful, and then act accordingly. That tragedies are "undeserved" means, among other things, that we cannot distinguish a clear causal relation (in terms of sufficient conditions) between any proposed line of action and the non-occurrence of a tragic event. Hence, we cannot mobilize the will to achieve and the courage of creativity to confront the possibility of tragedy.

Likewise, our sense of moral responsibility seems to be of little help here, as it is not a question of confronting the evil intentions of other agents. Tragedies occur in the form of disasters and deprivations, but we cannot perceive any agent responsible for them. Tragedies are *events*, rather than actions. Hence, we seem to have little use for the vocabulary of morality, which is typically adapted to the evaluation of actions and motives in terms of right and wrong, good and bad. However, as we well know, when we ourselves are the victims of tragedy, our inability to accept what has happened to us prompts us to dress our complaints in a quasi-moral language, asking for a justifying *reason* for our misfortune: "Why me?"

> When we suffer, our sufferings are not our fault, and so we deserve compensation. The underlying understanding is that we are entitled to a good life, a happy, healthy, comfortable life…. This may be the language of justice, but it is not the language of tragedy. (Solomon, p. 121.)

As Robert Solomon observes, our reactions to various forms of harm and suffering should be suited to their background. While it is sometimes appropriate to react with resentment and to demand compensation or exact retribution, on other occasions this is not really a reasonable response:

> Some things are within our control, and this is the proper sphere of justice. We live with others in a society such that people can be held responsible for what they do. Within that social context, we are right to be offended, angered, resentful, and even punitive when they cheat us. But we also live in and are sometimes confronted by an "indifferent" universe. This is a very different context. We say that nature "cheats" us, but we realize that we have now moved to the land of metaphor. Nature doesn't cheat. There is no one to blame. (Solomon, p. 122.)

But could not the courage of conviction, in a more indirect way, help us confront the fear of tragedy? We have already argued (in chapter 4) that a person may fortify herself against the fear of personal transience by reminding herself that she is an agent, and so mobilize a sense of dignity that will work also in those everyday contexts in which questions of moral duties and rights do not arise. This move is not fully satisfying when it comes to dealing with tragedy, however. The idea that tragedies are "undeserved" implies that while a tragic event may well deprive us of our capacity for agency, its occurrence is not itself controlled by anything we choose to do or not to do. Hence, since agency cannot prevent tragedy, reminding ourselves of our status as agents is not likely to be a sufficient antidote to a fear of tragedy.

However, this line of reasoning overlooks another indirect way of confronting this kind of fear that is also available within the framework of the theory of courage developed here. The fear of being a victim of tragic events, such as going through life unloved, or having a disabling illness, has its roots in the agent's awareness of (and terrified response to) the fact that life comes with no guarantees, not even regarding basic aspects of well-being. As we have already argued (in chapter 3), the courage of creativity rejects the kind of negative planning that is obsessed with looking for guarantees that nothing will go wrong. Implicit in this rejection is an acceptance of the fact that life is characterized by a certain amount of unpredictability. And to accept this fact is also to accept the possibility of tragedy. Hence, our theory supports Solomon's conclusion that "[t]he important thing is not to deny tragedy, but to embrace it as an essential part of the life we love and for which we should be so grateful" (Solomon, p. 144).

Having said this, however, we should take care not to get obsessed with the possibility of tragedy. To accept that possibility is one thing, to be dominated by it is to indulge in the negative planning rejected by the courage of creativity. Precisely because the possibility of tragedy cannot be eliminated by any amount of planning, we should not let it occupy too much space in our deliberations about the future. We should also remind ourselves that unpredictability is not exclusively of the tragic kind. After all, we may unexpectedly meet someone to love and to be loved by, and we may recover from what we thought to be a fatal illness. Unpredictability provides a reason not only for fear, but also for hope.

Moreover, we could try to balance our fear of becoming a victim of tragedy by turning our attention away from the prospects of our personal good and instead adopting a moral perspective, which includes our personal good, but is not limited to it. This is how the courage of conviction works. Of course, our sense of moral responsibility may not suffice to vanquish our fears of loneliness and of getting cancer, but these fears may at least be less powerful if our perspective is not exclusively self-centred in the first place, and if our focus is on our duty to contribute, rather than on the question "What will happen to me?" Serious dedication to one's civic community and to the universal community of all agents may hence have the beneficial side-effect of reducing the agent's anxiety for unpredictable tragedy. This dedication can be manifested in many different ways, according to the varying interests and capacities of different agents. Clarifying a philosophical problem, producing an imaginative and enlightening piece of artwork, working as a physician or a teacher, participating in humanitarian relief work, contributing to political debates and democratic processes – all these activities exemplify various ways in which an agent may transcend a self-centred preoccupation with her personal good and so minimize her exposure to the fear of being a victim of tragedy.

More specifically, to fortify ourselves against the fear of tragedy, we should develop a proper *sense of fairness*. That is, we should inculcate in ourselves an awareness of the fact that we all, as human persons, share a basic vulnerability. We are all mortal, and we may all be the victims of events that may cause us pain and disability. Hence, the possibility of tragedy is not something that afflicts only me or you. On the contrary, it is part of what it means to be human. There is no guarantee that the rich man will stand a better chance of being loved than the poor woman, and no matter what degree of success a person may have accomplished for herself, her life might be cut short by an unexpected illness or accident, and her good looks, or whatever aspect of herself she is proud of, may be lost without her being able to do anything to prevent this from happening.

We should accept our vulnerability (though we do not have to like it) as a part of our humanity. Why should we demand for ourselves a right to be excepted from that vulnerability that no other human can escape? What right do we have, being human persons, to complain about not being invulnerable? Such a complaint would indicate not only a lack of proper humility, but also a lack of fairness, as we seem to demand for ourselves a status that is denied by nature to our fellow men.

When we look around we will find that there are other human persons, as vulnerable as we are, who, although they are already suffering from the impact of a tragic loss or illness, still struggle on, trying to improve their lot and to contribute to the common good. We may find people who are already so victimized by tragedy that they are unable to make any but the smallest contribution, or perhaps must confine themselves simply to trying to get through another day – the little girl in a wheelchair, neurologically damaged from birth, the old woman suffering from osteoporosis, incapable of leaving her bed, and so on. Awareness of victims of tragedy like these should help us put our personal complaints in a different and wider perspective. We are not the only ones that suffer, and we should not presume that our suffering is of the worst possible kind. This is another aspect of fairness: we should not assume that we are the ones who have most reason to complain about our lot, given the wide range of misfortunes that actually afflict people. Whatever reason we may have to complain, be it our inability to find sexual love, or the loss of our youth, we are likely to find people who face much graver forms of adversity. Moreover, while we may fear that we *will be* the victims of tragedy, there are people who already *are* such victims, and yet they struggle on with their lives to the best of their abilities.

A proper sense of fairness should tell us that it is wrong for us to indulge in self-pity, while other people, who share with us the vulnerability of human beings, and who may already be the victims of tragedy, facing a lot more pain than we presently do, still do their best to cope and to contribute, engaging themselves in productive work, supporting their friends and neighbours, participating in political work, and so on. A proper sense of fairness should tell us that instead of the self-centred question "What will happen to me?", we should ask of ourselves: "How can I best contribute my share as a human being?" What right do we have to give up and to despair, when there are people, more unfortunate than we are, who still try to manage?

Perhaps the fear of being a victim of tragedy afflicts the self-centred person the most, as she is likely to be too swamped by personal concerns to get a reasonable and fair perspective of herself. Once we start to look around, however, comparing ourselves not only to those who are the most fortunate, but also to those who are worse off than we are, we may come to realize that we have less reason to complain about our lot than we thought at first. For all our lamentations about our bad luck, we are still likely to find many people who would gladly swop their lives with ours. Accepting our shared vulnerability as human beings, as well as our duty to do our fair share of contributions to the common good (of our civic community as well as of the universal community of all agents), could then constitute the basis of a more general form of courage, namely, *the courage to live the life of a human being*.

Moreover, this sense of fairness, based on our understanding of what it means to be a human being, has implications not only for our willingness to contribute to the common good, but also for our motivation to make something of our own lives. As we come to see how other persons, in spite of sometimes very adverse conditions of life, still have been successful in improving their lot, educating themselves, finding a stimulating and remunerative job, and so on, we are reminded of our own possibilities for improvement. If these people, under those circumstances, could do it, why would it be impossible for us to do the same? In this way, a proper sense of fairness, based on an understanding not only of the vulnerability, but also of the possibilities of a human life, may be supportive not only of the will to contribute, but also of the will to achieve. Hence, the courage to live the life of a human being and its underlying sense of fairness can be seen to include important motivational aspects of the courage of conviction as well as of the courage of creativity.

The conclusion of the present study is that the value of courage consists in its being a necessary means to individual self-fulfilment as well as to moral progress. The courage of creativity, with its emphasis on constructive creativity and positive planning, has an obvious prudential value as it supports the agent's resolution to go on with her plans and projects, in spite of obstacles and the possibility of failure. The courage of conviction, on the other hand, has a moral value when it is motivated by the agent's sense of moral responsibility for the generic rights of her recipients and for the maintenance of rights-protecting institutions, as it then will be instrumental to the promotion of a societal order characterized by justice and compassion.

This is not meant to deny that the exercise of courage can be problematic. If the courage of creativity is exercised by an agent without any regard for the generic rights of her recipients, it may well turn the agent's efficiency in achieving her goals into a ruthless pursuit of her personal good at the expense of the freedom and well-being of other people, their rights and interests being treated as just another obstacle to be overcome. And if the agent's sense of moral responsibility, which motivates her courage of conviction, does not recognize the generic right of all agents, but rather takes its point of departure in a theocratic or fascist view of the world, her courage will not contribute to the moral improvement of the world, but rather the opposite. We could, for instance, think of the fanatical morality of the extreme Islamists who on 11 September 2001 hijacked two aeroplanes and crashed them against the towers of the World Trade Center building in New York, thereby killing themselves and thousands of innocent people. The hijackers did possess the courage of conviction, but far from being an instrument of a justified morality, their courage assisted them in committing a terrible crime. In fact, when it comes to extremists who reject the idea of universal generic rights and who want to bring down the institutions of the civic community, we would prefer that they were cowards rather than courageous, since their courage is what makes them really dangerous to us.

Still, the fact that courage, in both of its forms, can be instrumental to morally reprehensible ends, does not entail that courage as such can or should be rejected. On the contrary, it takes courage to stand up to villains who themselves are courageous. And for any one of us to realize our aspirations for a good life, we will need at least some courage (of creativity) to overcome the obstacles and adversities that any human life is likely to contain.

The centrality of agency in our lives makes courage, in both of its forms, a necessary virtue. It is only by being able to mobilize our powers of agency that we can hope to create for ourselves lives that we can find worth living. Amartya Sen, for instance, has pointed to a significant relationship between enhancing the agency of women in developing countries and promoting their well-being:

> Empirical work in recent years has brought out very clearly how the relative respect and regard for women's well-being is strongly influenced by such variables as women's ability to earn an independent income, to find employment outside the home, to have ownership rights and to have literacy and be educated participants in decisions within and outside the family. Indeed, even the survival disadvantage of women compared with men in developing countries seems to go down sharply – and may even get eliminated – as progress is made in these agency aspects. (Sen, p. 191.)

A person who is unable to see herself as a successful agent and who instead has the image of herself as a helpless victim of external events and of the actions of other people, is unlikely to initiate a process whereby her conditions of life can be improved. To overcome such a low opinion of one's ability to realize one's projects, it takes a certain amount of the courage of creativity, whereby the agent enables herself to confront her fear of failure and so gains a basic confidence in her powers of agency. And to bring about an improvement of conditions of life not only at the personal level but also at the level of a whole community, it will take a certain amount of the courage of conviction, as such an improvement requires of the agent that she is capable of taking a stand on the issue of social rights. Hence, both forms of courage are required, for prudential as well as for moral reasons.

Moreover, by means of their relationship to agency, the courage of creativity and a morally justified courage of conviction may come to develop in a mutually supportive way in an agent. As the individual person awakens to her status as an agent and comes to recognize not only her capacity to create a good life for herself, but also the importance for that capacity of the generic goods of freedom and well-being, she will also be able to recognize the moral justification of a social order that protects these goods for all agents. Hence, she will be at least prima facie motivated to support such a social order. Consequently, as she develops in herself a sense of what it means to be an agent, the individual person may also develop a sense of moral responsibility which in turn may motivate a morally justified courage of conviction on her part. But to the extent that the agent, motivated by her sense of moral responsibility, involves herself in the support of rights-protecting institutions, she may also reinforce her self-esteem as an agent, as she comes to see that her contributions make a difference to the freedom and well-being of other agents. Accordingly, her will to achieve may gain strength from her other-regarding activities, and she may gain a new and stronger confidence in her powers of agency, which will contribute to her ability to confront her fear of failure as she sets out to realize her personal projects. Hence, as the agent develops a morally justified courage of conviction, she enables herself to develop a courage of creativity, and vice versa.

It is in our capacity as agents that we need courage, and it is from the point of view of agency that we should evaluate various manifestations of courage. Courage should not be thought of as the exclusive virtue of superior men whereby they are able to command the obedience of the multitude. Nor should it be thought of as an exclusively martial virtue, primarily the property of warriors. Instead it should be thought of as an important agency-supporting disposition, whereby each one of us increases his or her chances of a fulfilling life, and all of us increase our chances of living in communities that protect our generic rights.

Literature

Ambrose, Stephen E., *Undaunted Courage,* Touchstone, 1997
Anderson, Benedict, *Imagined Communities*, Verso, 1991
Andrée, S. A., "Förslag till polarfärd med luftballong", *Ymer*, vol. 15, pp. 55–70, 1895
Andrée, S. A., Strindberg, Nils, Frænkel, Knut, *Med Örnen mot polen*, Albert Bonniers Förlag, 1930
Aristotle, *Ethics*, Penguin Books, 1976
Bailey, Cyril (ed.), *Epicurus: The Extant Remains*, The Clarendon Press, 1926
Berlin, Isaiah, *Personal Impressions*, Penguin Books, 1982
Beyleveld, Deryck, *The Dialectical Necessity of Morality*, The University of Chicago Press, 1991
Boethius, *The Consolation of Philosophy*, Macmillan Publishing Company, 1962
Bomann-Larsen, Tor, *Roald Amundsen*, Cappelen, 1995
Bowlt, John E., "Body Beautiful", in Bowlt, John E. & Matich, Olga (eds.), *Laboratory of Dreams*, Stanford University Press, 1996
Callan, Eamonn, "Patience and Courage", *Philosophy*, vol. 68:266, pp. 523–540, 1993
Crichton, Paul, "A prescription for happiness?", *The Times Literary Supplement*, 2 July 1999
Dent, N. J. H., "The Value of Courage", *Philosophy*, vol. 56:218, pp. 574–577, 1981
Diogenes Laertius, *Lives of Eminent Philosophers*, vol. II, Loeb Classical Library, 1979
Ekholm, Nils, "Om väderleksförhållandena i norra polarområdet under sommaren, särskildt med afseende på den tilltänkta polarfärden i luftballong", *Ymer*, vol. 15, pp. 211–218, 1895
Emerson, Ralph Waldo, *The Collected Works of Ralph Waldo Emerson*, vol. II, The Belknap Press of Harvard University Press, 1979

Fogelman, Eva, *Conscience & Courage*, Cassell, 1995
Foot, Philippa, *Virtues and Vices and Other Essays in Moral Philosophy*, Basil Blackwell, 1978
Førde, Olav Helge, "Is Imposing Risk Awareness Cultural Imperialism?", *Social Science & Medicine*, vol. 47:9, pp. 1155–1159, 1998
Frankl, Viktor, *Man's Search For Meaning*, Washington Square Press, 1963
Furedi, Frank, *Culture of Fear*, Continuum, 2002
Gallo, Max, *L'homme Robespierre: Histoire d'une solitude*, Librairie Académique Perrin, 1968
Galston, William A., "Cosmopolitan Altruism", *Social Philosophy & Policy*, vol 10:1, pp. 118–134, 1993
Geach, Peter, *The Virtues*, Cambridge University Press, 1977
Gewirth, Alan, *Reason and Morality*, The University of Chicago Press, 1978
Gewirth, Alan, *Human Rights*, The University of Chicago Press, 1982
Gewirth, Alan, *The Community of Rights*, The University of Chicago Press, 1996
Gewirth, Alan, *Self-Fulfillment*, Princeton University Press, 1998
Goleman, Daniel, *Emotional Intelligence*, Bantam Books, 1995
Hallie, Philip, *Tales of Good and Evil, Help and Harm*, Harper Perennial, 1998
Hampson, Norman, *The Life and Opinions of Maximilien Robespierre*, Basil Blackwell, 1988
Hare, Richard, *Freedom and Reason*, Clarendon Press, 1963
Herodotus, vol. III, Loeb Classical Library, 1982
Hochschild, Adam, *King Leopold's Ghost*, Papermac, 2000
Human Development Report 1999 [Published for the United Nations Development Programme], Oxford University Press, 1999
Huntford, Roland, *Scott and Amundsen*, Hodder and Stoughton, 1979
Hursthouse, Rosalind, *On Virtue Ethics*, Oxford University Press, 1999
Kaye, Howard, L., "Cultural Being or Biological Being: The 'Implications' of Modern Biology", in Wesson, Robert & Williams, Patricia A. (eds.), *Evolution and Human Values*, Rodopi, 1995
Kennedy, John F., *Profiles in Courage*, Harper & Brothers, 1961

Kent, Susan Kingsley, *Making Peace: The Reconstruction of Gender in Interwar Britain*, Princeton University Press, 1993
MacIntyre, Alasdair, *After Virtue*, Duckworth, 1985
Mackie, John, *Ethics: Inventing Right and Wrong*, Penguin Books, 1977
Marcus Aurelius, *Meditations*, Oxford World's Classics, 1998
Marx, Karl, "Economic and Philosophical Manuscripts of 1844", in Marx, Karl & Engels, Frederick, *Collected Works*, volume 3, Lawrence & Wishart, 1975
McPherson, James M., *For Cause and Comrades*, Oxford University Press, 1997
Moody-Adams, Michele, *Fieldwork in Familiar Places*, Harvard University Press, 1997
Mosse, George, *Fallen Soldiers*, Oxford University Press, 1990
Nagel, Thomas, *The View From Nowhere*, Oxford University Press, 1986
Nietzsche, Friedrich, *The Will to Power*, Vintage Books, 1968
Nozick, Robert, *The Examined Life,* Touchstone, 1990
Österberg, Eva, "Förbjuden kärlek och förtigandets strategi: När Ulrika Eleonora gifte sig med Maria", in Österberg, Eva (ed.), *Jämmerdal & fröjdesal*, Atlantis, 1997
Putnam, Daniel, "Psychological Courage", *Philosophy, Psychiatry, & Psychology*, vol. 4:1, pp. 1–11, 1997
Rachman, Stanley, *Fear and Courage*, W. H. Freeman and Company, 1990
Rescher, Nicholas, *Ethical Idealism,* University of California Press, 1987
Resic, Sanimir, *American Warriors in Vietnam*, Doctoral Dissertation, Lund University, Sweden, 1999
Rials, Stéphane (ed.), *La déclaration des droits de l'homme et du citoyen*, Hachette, 1988
Ridley, Jasper, *Mussolini*, St. Martin's Press, 1998
Rorty, Amélie Oksenberg, "The Two Faces of Courage", *Philosophy*, vol. 61:236, pp. 151–172, 1986
de Rosa, Peter, *Rebels*, Poolbeg, 1996
Russell, Bertrand, *The Conquest of Happiness*, Routledge, 1993
Sen, Amartya, *Development as Freedom*, Oxford University Press, 1999

Seneca, *Ad Lucilium Epistulae Morales*, vols. I–III, Loeb Classical Library, 1970–79
Sharples, R. W., *Stoics, Epicureans and Sceptics*, Routledge, 1996
Sidgwick, Henry, *The Methods of Ethics*, Hackett Publishing Company, 1981
Singer, Irving, *The Creation of Value*, The Johns Hopkins University Press, 1996
Singer, Peter, *The Expanding Circle*, Oxford University Press, 1981
Skinner, B. F., *Beyond Freedom and Dignity*, Alfred A. Knopf, 1971
Solomon, Robert C., *The Joy of Philosophy*, Oxford University Press, 1999
Sundman, Per Olof, *Ingen fruktan, intet hopp*, Bonniers, 1968
Tamarin, Alfred (ed.), *Benjamin Franklin: An Autobiographical Portrait*, Macmillan, 1969
Taylor, Charles, *The Ethics of Authenticity*, Harvard University Press, 1991
Taylor, Philip M., *Munitions of the Mind*, Manchester University Press, 1995
Thomas, Evan, *Robert Kennedy: His Life*, Simon & Schuster, 2000
Todorov, Tzvetan, *Facing the Extreme*, Owl Books, 1997
Turner, Victor, *The Forest of Symbols*, Cornell University Press, 1970
Wallace, James D., *Virtues and Vices*, Cornell University Press, 1978
Walton, Douglas N., *Courage: A Philosophical Investigation*, University of California Press, 1986
Walzer, Michael, *Just and Unjust Wars*, Basic Books, 1992
Warwick, Kevin, *In the Mind of the Machine*, Arrow Books, 1998
Weber, Max, *The Protestant Ethic and the Spirit of Capitalism*, Routledge, 1992
Wilson, Edward O., "Consilience Among the Great Branches of Learning", *Dædalus*, vol. 127:1, pp. 131–149, 1998
Wolf, Susan, "Happiness and Meaning: Two Aspects of the Good Life", *Social Philosophy & Policy*, vol. 14:1, pp. 207–225, 1997
Wood, Charles T., *Joan of Arc and Richard III*, Oxford University Press, 1988

von Wright, Georg Henrik, *The Varieties of Goodness*, Routledge & Kegan Paul, 1963
Wurtzel, Elizabeth, *Prozac Nation*, Riverhead Books, 1995
Yarwood, Doreen, *The Architecture of Europe*, Spring Books, 1987

Index

agency, necessary goods of 99
agent, the importance of being an 22, 46, 65–66, 75–76, 98, 202–204
alienation 14–15
Amundsen, Roald 180–185
Andrée, Salomon August 167–180
Aristotle 43–44, 47, 70, 81–82, 180
autonomy 24–28

behaviourism 24–26
Berlin, Isaiah 23, 58
biologistic reductionism 19–21
Boethius 77
Brittain, Vera 191
Brooke, Rupert 23

Callan, Eamonn 48–49
caring, ordinary virtue of 155–161
Clark, William 63, 120
common good,
   causal and normative theses of the 114
   civic dimension of the 112
   universal dimension of the 112
   positive and normative conceptions of the 110
communitarians 113–115
community,
   morally contingent and morally necessary forms of 108
   civic 108–110, 111–113
   universal 112–113

confidence, development of 47
constructive creativity, principle of 48
courage,
   and insensitivity 192–195
   and sexism 187–192
   and tragedy 195–201
   not necessarily a moral virtue 32–39
   of conviction 61–90
   of creativity 45–59
   relation between the two forms of 132–136, 201–204
   to live the life of a human being 201
Crichton, Paul 10–11
curiosity 52

danger 30–32, 40
degrees of needfulness for action, criterion of 103, 155
Dent, N. J. H. 187–192
depersonalization 16
depression 10–11
destructive creativity, principle of 54
dignity,
   of an autonomous agent 75
   of a moral agent 74
   ordinary virtue of 155–156, 159
dying, fear of 70–84

Emerson, Ralph Waldo 82–83
enlightened citizenship 116–117
Epicurus 80–81

failure, fear of 29
fairness, sense of 199
fear 29–32
Fogelman, Eva 67, 135–136, 161–164, 188–189
Foot, Philippa 37–38
Førde, Olav Helge 55–56
Frankl, Viktor 79
Franklin, Benjamin 57–58
Furedi, Frank 18

Galston, William 61
Geach, Peter 27
Generic Consistency, Principle of 100
Gewirth, Alan 7, 42, 57, 75–76, 99–105, 109, 145, 165–166
Goleman, Daniel 11, 13, 20–21, 49–50, 57
Gray, J. Glenn 146–147

Hallie, Philip 88–89, 160–161
Hare, Richard 27
heroism,
 of honour 142–145, 154–155, 161
 of responsibility 142–145, 154–155, 161–166
Hursthouse, Rosalind 39, 44
Hänsch, Anja 8, 18

individualism 22–26
intervening action, principle of the 165

Jefferson, Thomas 120, 125
Joan of Arc 190
Johnson, Andrew 85–88

Kaye, Howard 19, 21
Kennedy, John F. 34, 84–88
Kennedy, Robert 83–84

Lewis, Meriwether 63, 119–126
liminality 18
Lucretius 72

MacIntyre, Alasdair 39, 114–115
Mackie, John 28
Marcus Aurelius 78
Marx, Karl 14–15
McPherson, James 64, 149–154, 191
meaninglessness, fear of 65–69, 116–118
Mussolini, Benito 188–190

Nagel, Thomas 68–69, 92–104
negative planning 53
Nozick, Robert 65–66

objective agent-self 100–106
objective self 73–74, 91–106
optimism,
 agency-related 47
 attitudinal 51

Pearse, Patrick 71
personal transience, fear of 29
positive actualism 50
positive planning 47
positive possibilism 50
prudence, objection from 174
prudential assessment of courage 179
Putnam, Daniel 46–47

INDEX

Rachman, Stanley 54
Read, Herbert 23
Rescher, Nicholas 51
Resic, Sanimir 148
Robespierre, Maximilien 126–132
Rommel, Erwin 35–36
Roosevelt, Franklin Delano 58
Rorty, Amélie Oksenberg 68, 142, 185–186, 192–193
Ross, Edmund G. 85–87
Russell, Bertrand 57

Schindler, Oskar 162
Scott, Sir Robert 180–185
Sen, Amartya 202–203
Seneca 78–79
Sidgwick, Henry 84, 144
Singer, Irving 65
Singer, Peter 107
Skinner, B. F. 24–25
social death, fear of 84–89
Solomon, Robert 197–198

Stålhammar, Ulrika Eleonora 190–191
Stanley, Henry 133–134

Taylor, Charles 12
Todorov, Tzvetan 137–147, 155–160
Turner, Victor 18

Wallace, James D. 31
Walzer, Michael 194
Walton, Douglas 30, 34–37, 43, 146–147
Warwick, Kevin 13–14
Weber, Max 14
Wilson, Edward O. 19–20
Wolf, Susan 66
von Wright, Georg Henrik 37, 42
Wurtzel, Elizabeth 10

Xerxes 55